The Paraguayan War

A Captivating Guide to a South American War Called the War of the Triple Alliance between Paraguay and the Allied Countries of Argentina, Brazil, and Uruguay

Free Bonus from Captivating History (Available for a Limited time)

Hi History Lovers!

Now you have a chance to join our exclusive history list so you can get your first history ebook for free as well as discounts and a potential to get more history books for free! Simply visit the link below to join.

Captivatinghistory.com/ebook

Also, make sure to follow us on Facebook, Twitter and Youtube by searching for Captivating History.

Table of Contents

Introduction

The Paraguayan War of 1864 to 1870 is not well known outside of South America. It was a major war between the alliance of Argentina, Brazil, and Uruguay against Paraguay. The war nearly obliterated Paraguay. But to understand the war, it is helpful to learn about the political and social dynamics of the place and time. That includes learning about the rivalry between the Spanish and Portuguese empires, how Brazil and Argentina inherited the empires' quarrels, and the differences in how Spanish and Portuguese colonies achieved independence. It also helps to know a bit about the unusual geography of the great rivers and plains of South America and how cattle went wild and gave rise to a culture of ranching and frontier cowboys called gauchos. It helps to know about the history of the Jesuits and their creation of a kind of theocratic state in what is now Paraguay.

The Paraguayan War is also known as the War of the Triple Alliance because Argentina, Brazil, and Uruguay formed an alliance against Paraguay. To this day, more than 150 years later, the war remains the bloodiest conflict between Latin American nations. With the exception of the Crimean War (1853–1856), the Paraguayan War might have been the bloodiest war between nations anywhere on Earth in the century between the fall of Napoleon and the outbreak of the First World War. Several internal civil wars and some rebellions in China did have higher casualties, though.

The story of how the war came about and how it was conducted involves a number of fascinating larger-than-life characters, among them three ruthless dictators of Paraguay, including one of the most unique autocrats in human history; Pedro I and Pedro II, who were emperors of Brazil; a number of *caudillos* (military dictators) in Argentina and Uruguay; a Brazilian aristocrat who turned out to be a great strategist; and one of the most remarkable love stories of all time between an Irish woman and a Paraguayan tyrant.

An important part of the story of this war is the aftermath. We will explore how a small nation survived the catastrophe and how this bloody conflict has left a permanent mark on all four of the countries involved. This book will guide you through this remarkable and entirely captivating history.

Chapter 1 – Geography and Rival Empires

Paraguay is a smaller nation, landlocked deep in the interior of South America. Its history is one of being a buffer zone in the disputed territory between the Spanish and Portuguese colonial empires. After its independence, it served as a buffer between Brazil and Argentina. Paraguay's "small" size is relative to its giant neighbors, Argentina and Brazil. Paraguay measures around 157,000 square miles and is considerably larger than Japan and Germany.

Much of Paraguay is located in the region sometimes called the Plata, Plate, or La Plata region, named after the great river, Río de la Plata, that results from the confluence of two other great rivers, the Uruguay and the Paraná. The Plata is largely an estuary and joins the South Atlantic; it is more than a hundred miles wide at its mouth. The entire La Plata River system covers well over a million square miles of land.

A map of the La Plata basin.

The name "La Plata" may have come from the silver that once was transported downriver from the fabulously rich silver mines of Potosí in Upper Peru (now Bolivia). Argentina also takes its name from the Latin word for silver, *argentum*, which is thought to refer to the sun reflecting off the mass of water, as it looks like silver. Buenos Aires, the capital of Argentina, is on the west bank of the Plata estuary, and Montevideo, the capital of Uruguay, is on the east bank; they are a little more than one hundred miles apart. The name Buenos Aires apparently refers to good air, that is, good winds for sailing.

These great rivers are an essential part of Paraguayan history and have much to do with the war this book describes, largely because they are navigable. The Paraguay is 1,500 miles long, half of which either flows through Paraguay or forms part of its borders. At 2,900 miles in length, the Paraná is the longer river but is considerably less navigable. Both rivers are subject to large fluctuations in water levels.

The Paraguay tends to frequently alter its course, and at the time of the Paraguayan War, the river was characterized by oxbow lakes, braided meanders, river islands, shifting sandbars, and riverside swamps.[1]

The river systems are navigable for ocean-going ships for hundreds of miles inland and are navigable for smaller ships for more than 1,600 miles into the interior, almost to the Bolivian Andes. The rivers historically were the principal outlets for trade from Upper Peru (now Bolivia) and Paraguay. The inland river route was important to Portuguese Brazil and to independent Brazil, as it was the easiest route to the interior province of Mato Grosso, where substantial mineral wealth was found in the 1700s. The dangerous overland trip to Mato Grosso by mule and canoe took months.[2]

Asunción, the capital of Paraguay, is almost nine hundred miles upriver from Buenos Aires, located where the Pilcomayo River flows into the Paraguay. The Paraguay later joins the Paraná, and the Paraná and the Uruguay unite to form the La Plata River. The Paraná begins in the interior Brazilian province of Mata Grosso, and the Pilcomayo originates in the jungles and mountains of Bolivia. The Uruguay River rises in the interior of Brazil's south and flows southwest before it joins the Paraná.

Rivers form a sizable part of the borders of all four Plata countries. A crucial historical element is that Mato Grosso was conveniently reachable only by the rivers, so the Portuguese and then Brazil insisted on navigation rights to reach the remote province, particularly after gold was discovered there in the 1700s.

Paraguay is not just a land of rivers and swamps, though. There are hills and mountainous terrain to the east of Asunción, where the end of the war happened. In the north and west, there are mostly unsettled plains and forested lands. Most of the war took place in the south of the country that borders Argentina and Brazil.

---

[1] Hanratty, Dana and Meditz, Sandra. *Paraguay: A Country Study.* Washington, DC: Library of Congress, 1988.

[2] Shipping Wonders of the World. "Rio de la Plata."
https://www.shippingwondersoftheworld.com/river_plate.html Retrieved January 14, 2023.

Asunción was founded in 1537. For many years, the city was more important than Buenos Aires, which was founded a year prior. The second founding of Buenos Aires in 1580 gradually lessened Asunción's importance, particularly after Buenos Aires became the capital of the new Viceroyalty of La Plata in the 1770s (the first founding of Buenos Aires in 1536 failed). Buenos Aires assessed taxes and tolls and deliberately reduced the importance of other cities and towns, including Asunción. The other great city on the La Plata River, Montevideo, was not founded until 1724 when the Spanish decided a settlement was needed on the east bank of the La Plata estuary to counter the Portuguese expanding from southern Brazil.

Paraguay was always remote from the centers of authority, whether the viceroy was seated in Lima or Buenos Aires, and was accustomed to a lot of local autonomy. The colonists in Asunción threw out more than one governor and were in a state of rebellion more than once. The settlers around Asunción also strongly disliked the Jesuit-controlled settlements of the Guaraní people to their east. Much of Paraguay also remained a frontier region, subject to occasional raids from indigenous people in the northern settlements well into the 1800s.

For much of the Spanish colonial era, the Plata region was a little more than a backwater. The Spanish were much more interested in Mexico and Peru, which had far denser indigenous populations that supplied labor for plantations and mines. The vastly productive silver mines in Mexico and Upper Peru supplied Spain with a huge amount of wealth and enabled the Spanish to finance wars with the Ottoman Turks in the Mediterranean and to fight the rise of Protestantism in Europe. The wealth carried across the Atlantic in the annual silver fleets financed Spain's *Siglo de Oro* (Spain's Golden Century).

American silver also financed the famed *tercios*, Spanish troop formations that dominated the battlefields of Europe for more than a century. The silver helped finance the Spanish Armada's mission against England in 1588. Large amounts of silver were smuggled out of the La Plata River, but little is known of who it enriched.

A second very important environmental aspect is that the regions watered by the rivers in their lower courses include several hundred thousand square miles of fine grazing land, such as the Pampas in Argentina. The region did not have any large herds of predominant grazers, such as, for example, the herds of bison in the Great Plains of North America. However, once cattle were introduced, some went wild. The result was a spectacular explosion of herds of feral cattle owned by no one. Horses also escaped and went wild, allowing some of the indigenous people to develop a horse nation culture similar to the Sioux and Comanche in North America. These horseback warriors became extremely formidable as a military force and were able to resist settlement in much of the interior of Argentina and the south of Chile until the 1880s.

The huge herds of feral cattle gradually began to supply a trade based on cattle hides. At first, the carcass was left to rot, but methods of drying meat were developed. The salted and sun-dried meat was called *charqui* (which is the origin of the American term beef jerky). There are a number of similarities between this history and the history of Mexican California, where feral cattle supplied an export industry of hides and tallow. Californian history intersected with traders from New England, as described in New England sailor Richard Henry Dana's 1840 *Two Years Before the Mast*. Dana's book describes an economy and society broadly similar to the Pampas and adjacent areas. The Plata hide trade was much larger, lasted much longer, and involved British merchants instead of Americans like Dana.

Dried meat became a large export from the Plata, supplementing the trade in hides. It was used to feed sailors and soldiers in the centuries before refrigeration and was sold in Brazil and Cuba as food for slaves. The dried meat did more than enrich merchants; it also led to the creation of a cowboy culture that was every bit as rich as the cowboy culture of the American West. This was the origin of the fabled gaucho frontier culture in Argentina, which extended from the Pampas to most of Uruguay and into much of the province of Rio Grande do Sul in southern Brazil.

The gauchos—cowboys—were mixed in origin, and many of them were mixed race. Some were descended from escaped slaves or natives. Sometimes, they were escapees from prisons or lived in exile. They were the labor force that herded the cattle and was often exploited by merchants and others who had enough money and political clout to claim land to form ranches. The gauchos were stereotyped as lazy, illiterate, dirty, violent, and free. For more than a century, the gauchos, whether they spoke Spanish, Portuguese, or

Guaraní, formed the cavalry forces that fought the natives, each other, and for independence. They formed much of the cavalry participating in the Paraguayan War. Several men from this culture rose to become powerful *caudillos.*

Another unique resource that was particularly important for Paraguay as a producer and for the other three countries as a consumer product was yerba mate. Yerba mate is a common drink throughout the Southern Cone of South America (the southernmost areas of the continent) and is much like coffee since it contains significant amounts of caffeine. It was used by the Guaraní long before the arrival of the Spanish. Yerba mate is brewed like tea and is traditionally sipped through a silver straw from a container made from a gourd. One cultural difference between the gauchos of the Pampas and the cowboys of the North American West is that the gauchos drank mate while the cowboys drank coffee. A gaucho's few possessions often included a fancy gourd bottle and straw for sipping mate.

Yerba mate is related to holly and takes the form of a bush. The leaves are plucked, much like tea harvesting, dried, and then sold. The species is related to the yaupon holly that was used by several of the Native Americans in the US Southeast, most famously as the Cherokee "black drink," which was used as a purgative in various ceremonies. Historically, it was used by the Guaraní people, the gaucho herders on the plains, and miners in Mato Grosso in Brazil. Yerba mate grew wild in the jungle parts of Paraguay and was a major export to Argentina and Brazil. Its close association with Paraguay can be seen in its Latin name, *Ilex paraguariensis.*[3]

For much of the Spanish colonial period, the Plata area was an unimportant part of the Spanish Empire. It was also of minor significance for the Portuguese colony. The Plata region was of some significance partly because it was a route for smuggling silver out of Upper Peru and smuggling goods into Upper Peru. The usual route for silver went to Lima and to ports on the Pacific for shipment to Panama. Silver would be unloaded there, then carried by mule train to a port in the Caribbean and transferred to the annual fleet to Spain.

[3] Wikipedia. "Yerba Mate." en.wikipedia.org/wiki/Yerba-mate/. Retrieved January 22, 2023.

Imported goods generally came by the same routes but in reverse.

It is unknown how much silver illicitly made its way by mule and boat downriver to Buenos Aires or what volume of goods was illicitly shipped upriver to avoid import taxes. It was a significant enough loss of tax revenue to cause concern for the authorities in Spain and the colonies. The smugglers were both Spanish and British. The British maintained a lively interest in Buenos Aires and the whole La Plata region in the 18th century.

In 1776, Spain revamped the region's government. Previously, Paraguay, the Plata region, and the contested territory of Uruguay had been administered as part of the Viceroyalty of Peru, with the capital being far away in Lima. The Viceroyalty of La Plata was set up in 1776 and based in Buenos Aires. The Plata region had gradually become more important as an outlet from Peru and for the local exports of hides, timber, tobacco, and yerba mate. Paraguay came under the administrative responsibility of the new viceroyalty, although it continued to supply Upper Peru with timber, mules, tobacco, and yerba mate and also continued to be a conduit for the smuggling of silver.[4]

A particularly unsettled part of the greater La Plata region was Mato Grosso, which long remained a frontier region and was contested by Spain and Portugal. With the discovery of gold there in 1725, the difficulty of communication between Mato Grosso and the rest of the Portuguese colony vastly increased, with the Portuguese insisting on their right to navigate up the Paraguay river system. The overland route to Mato Grosso and other regions in the interior was difficult, and some of the indigenous tribal peoples were warlike. A large number of Portuguese miners and colonists trying to reach these interior frontier regions were killed while fighting with the tribes.

The tribes posed a serious threat in the northern reaches of Paraguay as well. Asunción was concerned with the double threat of native raids to the north and the Portuguese interest in acquiring Paraguay. There were occasional skirmishes between Spanish forces and Portuguese troops on the Mato Grosso border. Sometimes, the

---

[4] Whigham, Thomas. *The Paraguayan War: Causes and Early Conduct*, 2nd Edition. Calgary, Alberta: University of Calgary Press, 2018, 17-20.

Portuguese skirmishers included natives who had allied with them. The Spanish authorities tried to encourage settlement in the north to establish a better claim and to enlarge the militia. After the expulsion of the Jesuits from the entire Spanish Empire in 1767, the Jesuit-Guaraní settlements no longer functioned as a screen against Portuguese pressure.[5]

[5] Williams, John. "The Undrawn Line: Three Centuries of Strife on the Paraguayan- Mato Grosso Border." *Luso-Brazilian Studies* 17 (1), Summer 1980. 23-25. JSTOR access January 24, 2023.

Chapter 2 – The Jesuits and the *Treinta Pueblos* in Paraguay

Paraguayan history contains one highly unusual element: the creation of semi-autonomous Jesuit theocracies ruling large populations of Guaraní indigenous people, almost as if they were created by and ruled by philosopher kings. These missions lasted for several generations and had an incalculable impact on Paraguay long after their existence. The imprint is thought to have had some serious cultural consequences, possibly including a predisposition to accept authoritarian rule.

Catholic religious orders penetrated into what is now Paraguay and the areas around it in search of souls to save for God and for converts to establish godly communities for the natives. The Franciscans were first, settling there in the 16th century, and then came the Jesuits in the early 17th century. The Jesuits established a thoroughly remarkable area of settlements called the *Treinta Pueblos de la Misiones*, thirty mission settlements that were mostly for the Guaraní people, who later came to be the majority population of Paraguay. In most of Spanish America, religious orders tried to settle nomadic or semi-nomadic tribes in mission settlements to better control them and ensure they remained Catholic once they converted. These Jesuit settlements became famous in Europe. At their peak, in about 1732,

---

these Jesuit settlements contained an estimated 140,000 natives.[6]

The two orders differed in how they built their missions. The Franciscans built missions for settling the converted indigenous peoples, but they were not designed to be autonomous the way the Jesuit communities were. Natives from the Franciscan missions served as laborers and provided the colony with loggers, teamsters, and harvesters of yerba mate from the forests. The Franciscan effort in Paraguay was in the general region of Asunción. The Jesuit colonies were farther in the interior and were, by design, autonomous and intentionally isolated the natives from Spanish and Portuguese influence. The Jesuits sought to protect their Guaraní converts from the evils of the world by keeping them separate.[7]

The interaction between the Jesuits and the Guaraní lasted for the better part of two centuries, creating a culture that was unique in the Americas. The Jesuits were trained in theology, languages, and how to win converts. They were often also trained in practical crafts, such as carpentry and architecture, that they could use to build missions. The Jesuits were an important part of the development of natural science in Europe for several centuries, as the Jesuits in other parts of the world reported to the Jesuit authorities in Europe about their failures and successes, about the plants and animals of the areas they evangelized in, and about the people they sought to convert. Letters and journals from the Jesuits and their missions all over the world now form vital resources for historians. The order was active in places as different and as far apart as Ethiopia, Angola, Goa, China, Japan, and Southeast Asia, but the thirty missions in Paraguay were unique.

In the thirty Jesuit communities, natives were not simply converted to Catholicism. They also formed village communities centered around a plaza, which was, in turn, centered on the church in the common Spanish style. Settling the natives was a deliberate effort to eliminate migration and seasonal movements that were typical of

---

[6] Rahmeier, Clarissa Sanfelice. "The Materiality of Cultural Encounters in the *Treinta Pueblos de la Missiones.*" Pages 69-70 in Linda A. Nelson, ed., *Cultural Worlds of the Jesuits in Colonial Latin America.* London: University of London Press, 2020.

[7] Whigham, Thomas. *The Paraguayan War: Causes and Early Conduct,* 2nd Edition. Calgary, Alberta: University of Calgary Press, 2018, 12-14.

hunter-gatherer cultures.

The indigenous people were also trained in crafts and produced a variety of necessities and items for trade. Many of the natives labored in workshops that were often located near the central plaza. The workshops produced tiles, bricks, pottery, and many other items. In each mission, some of the natives were responsible for planting and harvesting, while others produced crafts. Everyone contributed to the settlement's self-sufficiency.

The Jesuits brought most of the particulars of Spanish agriculture to the region, including chickens, sheep, goats, pigs, cattle, donkeys, and horses, as well as wheat, other grains, vegetables, and orchards. They brought the potter's wheel, printing, blacksmithing, and gunpowder too. In a settlement, four or five clergymen might minister to and govern several thousand natives.[8]

These theocratic communities expected the native converts to be almost constantly at either work or devotions. Adults were expected to learn about the Bible and attend Mass each day. There was a semblance of schools for the children, with catechism more likely taught than literacy. The indigenous people were supposed to learn Spanish, wear Spanish-style clothing, and abandon traditional religious practices. How well the communities actually lived up to what the Franciscans and Jesuits wanted is not known. It seems that the Guaraní formed a hybrid culture, incorporating Spanish elements but retaining some of their pre-conquest traditions and their language. As an example, the workshops used the Spanish potter's wheel to produce pottery to sell, but women continued to make pottery the traditional way by hand, using coils of clay to build pots.[9]

This may sound like an attempt to create a kind of theocratic paradise, but there was a highly dangerous factor in the lives of these communities and their residents. The thirty missions were in the border region between the Portuguese and the Spanish empires. The colonial Portuguese from the region of São Paulo were expanding

---

[8] Rahmeier, Clarissa Sanfelice. "The Materiality of Cultural Encounters in the *Treinta Pueblos de la Missiones*." Page 73 in Linda A. Nelson, ed., *Cultural Worlds of the Jesuits in Colonial Latin America*. London: University of London Press, 2020.

[9] Ibid, pg. 74.

---

inland, and they needed slaves for labor on plantations and in the mines. African slaves were brought from Angola, also a Portuguese colony, to Brazil, but there were not enough of them, and enslaving natives filled the need for slave labor.

For more than a century, raiders from Brazil, sometimes called *mamelucos* and sometimes called *bandeirantes*, conducted raids deep into the interior in search of natives to enslave. Some of the raids covered thousands of miles and were part of what gave Brazil its strong claim to so much of the interior of the continent. These raiders also dislocated many of the indigenous peoples and threatened the natives in the *Treinta Pueblos.*[10]

These Jesuit colonies offered considerable safety from the Brazilian slave raids. The Jesuits asked permission from the Spanish authorities to arm their natives, which was granted. This was highly unusual because the Spanish were justifiably wary of native rebellions. But without arms to resist the slave hunters from Brazil, the communities would probably have been destroyed. This experience of forming communities ruled by paternalistic leaders, together with the ability to defend themselves from dangerous outsiders, may be related to the later ability of authoritarian Paraguayan leaders to completely mobilize its population for defense, as López did in the Paraguayan War.

In 1750, representatives from Portugal and Spain met in Madrid to try to hammer out an agreement on who ruled what in the La Plata region. La Plata had become increasingly significant. The two governments agreed that all land east of the Uruguay River was to go to Portugal. Spain obtained Portuguese recognition of its title to the river port of Colonia del Sacramento in Uruguay, on the opposite side of the La Plata estuary from Buenos Aires. The agreement also forced thousands of Guaraní in the Spanish Jesuit colonies to leave the territory, as it now belonged to the Portuguese. Thousands of them refused to leave and began a stubborn resistance that amounted to a small war, lasting from 1753 to 1756.[11]

---

[10] Ibid

[11] Whigham, Thomas. *The Paraguayan War: Causes and Early Conduct*, 2ⁿᵈ Edition. Calgary, Alberta: University of Calgary Press, 2018, 17-18.

The resistance in that war was one of the excuses Spain used to throw the Jesuits out of its colonial empire. The Jesuits were expelled from Portugal and the Portuguese Empire in 1759. King Carlos III of Spain expelled the Jesuits from Spain and the Spanish Empire in 1767, and they were formally disbanded by Pope Clement XIV in 1773.

The repression of the Jesuits was part of an administrative overhaul of the entire Spanish Empire, which was brought about by the new Bourbon dynasty, which was related to the Bourbon dynasty in France. The Bourbons brought new and more efficient French methods of rule to Spain. The de facto independence of the Jesuit colonies in Paraguay was seen as a challenge to the Spanish administrators in the viceregal capitals, so the Jesuits had to go. Oddly, the Jesuits were protected in both Protestant Prussia and Orthodox Russia.

The historical impact of the Jesuits on Paraguay was important, and they functioned to prevent the Guaraní people from fragmenting under the continual slave raids from Brazil. Their cultural impact was considerable, but the overall impact remains a fiercely debated topic by historians. One view is that the centuries of Jesuit settlement shaped much of Paraguay's character, imprinting a Guaraní identity on Paraguay. Another view is that the Jesuits were paternalistic and created Paraguayan traits of dependency on autocratic leaders, which predisposed them to tyrants like Francia and the two López dictators. Still, another view is that the missions built a distinctive identity, one that was different from either the Spanish or the Portuguese, that allowed Paraguay to better resist both of them.

Chapter 3 – Breaking Away from Spain and Portugal

The conflict between the Portuguese and Spanish American colonies dated back to the 17th century when the São Paulo frontier *bandeirantes* conducted ceaseless expeditions of exploration and slave-raiding into the interior. The Jesuits armed their Guaraní protégés and formed them into military companies to resist frontier slave raids. There were other issues. The Portuguese had found diamonds and gold in the remote Mato Grosso, and it could far more readily be reached by travel upriver than by a long and difficult trip overland. Portugal wanted to control these routes.

The emergence of massive herds of feral cattle on the plains created a new economy of hides and dried meat. It also formed a new region for confrontation, as herders moved from Brazil's Rio Grande do Sul into Uruguay at the same time that herders filtered in from the Argentine Pampas into Uruguay.

To fully understand the Paraguayan War, it will help to visualize an era when populations were far smaller than today. Most people in most places lived in towns or rural settlements. Even the cities like Buenos Aries that were considered huge then would be considered small today. The participants in the Paraguayan War were the same nations as today, but in some ways, they were vastly different. Most obviously, populations in 1864 were only a fraction of what they are today. Brazil was the giant in the region, with about ten million people. The various provinces making up Argentina had something over a million inhabitants, and Uruguay had several hundred thousand. The size of Paraguay's population is disputed, but most historians think it was somewhere in the range of a half million.

The Paraguayan War was partially a result of the collapse of Spanish and Portuguese rule in the Americas. The colonial rivalry never solved the status of the borderlands between them. Newly independent Buenos Aires immediately declared itself to be the heir of the Spanish colony and claimed all the lands that were formerly part of the Viceroyalty of La Plata: the La Plata provinces, all of Paraguay and Uruguay, and most of Bolivia. After becoming independent in 1822, Brazil considered itself an heir to all of the Portuguese claims to Uruguay, Paraguay, and the interior frontier.

Independence in the Americas was closely connected to the Napoleonic Wars in Europe (1803–1815). Both Spain and Portugal had long since ceased to be powerful empires and had become minor military powers in Europe. They became increasingly unable to fully protect their colonies and even themselves from the claims of Britain and France. Napoleon's boundless ambition for an empire came to include incorporating Spain and Portugal into a continent dominated by the French.

In June 1806, the British, concerned about possible French intrusion, landed a force that occupied Buenos Aires for a year and a half. The Argentines gathered a force of about 8,000 volunteers, who drove the 1,500 British out of the city and the province. The British took refuge in Montevideo. They were protected by the Royal Navy, but the Uruguayans proved equally hostile. The episode proved that colonial forces could defeat professional soldiers and that a navy was a good idea. In a kind of ironic twist, the Argentinians were led by Santiago de Liniers, who was born in France and had served in the Spanish Navy.[12]

Napoleon invaded Spain in the fall of 1807, beginning a long and sanguinary portion of the Napoleonic Wars called the Peninsular War, which lasted from 1807 to 1814. The war devastated Spain and

---

[12] Whigham, Thomas. *The Paraguayan War: Causes and Early Conduct*, 2nd Edition. Calgary, Alberta: University of Calgary Press, 2018, 22-24.

parts of Portugal. Napoleon forced Spanish King Carlos IV to abdicate in favor of his son, who became Ferdinand VII (r. 1808, 1813–1833). In a complicated diplomatic maneuver, Napoleon removed Ferdinand VII from the Spanish throne and installed his own brother, Joseph Bonaparte, as king (r. 1808–1813).

Spain fractured into pro-French and anti-French factions, with several military governments organizing and competing to lead the resistance against French occupation. The most powerful of the juntas, the resistance governments, was the one established in Seville; it obtained British support. The authorities in the colonies had difficulty determining who ruled in Spain and what authority they had in the empire.[13]

A British force commanded by the duke of Wellington (later the victor of Waterloo) landed in Portugal and then invaded Spain. The Peninsular War came to involve British, Spanish, and Portuguese troops, which fought Napoleon's polyglot army (which contained troops from not only France but also Italy, the German lands, Poland, the Netherlands, and even Croatia). The Spanish who supported Joseph Bonaparte fought with the Spanish who backed Ferdinand. The decision of who should rule Spain became problematic.

In the Peninsular War, there were battles between regular army forces, but much of the fighting descended into a remarkably savage guerrilla war. This brutal war killed tens of thousands of French, British, Portuguese, and Spanish troops. It also cost the lives of tens of thousands of civilians. It devastated the countryside, disrupted trade, destroyed villages and towns, and sometimes descended into utter brutality. Perhaps the best evocation of the chaos and murderous warfare of the Peninsular War is the set of prints done by the Spanish painter Francisco Goya called *The Disasters of War*, which was created between 1810 and 1820. Goya's stark depictions of brutality in these prints retain the power to shock the observer more than two hundred years later.

---

[13] Ibid, pgs. 24-25.

One of eighty-two prints that Goya created of the war. This one depicts an elderly woman wielding a knife to defend a woman being harassed by a soldier.

Another casualty of the Peninsular War was Spanish control over its American colonies. The colonial administrators and Spanish loyalists in the colonies did not know who was in control of Spain. The sheer distance meant that the colonies were slow to learn of events in Europe. It took weeks to hear of victories and defeats. The Argentine militia throwing a small British army out of Buenos Aires showed that the colonial population could put together formidable military forces. But to what Spanish faction did loyalists in the colonies owe their loyalty? In the end, most of the loyalists and the actual Spanish troops and administrators in the colonies declared their support for the dethroned Ferdinand VII.

The severe weakening of Spanish control led to disputes among the various colonies. A sizable portion of the educated classes was influenced by the French Enlightenment, and many of them came to dispute the legitimacy of Spanish rule. The wars of independence in South America from 1810 to about 1825 were as violent and cruel as those in Spain, although they were smaller in scale and far larger in geographical extent. A small army of liberators under General José de San Martín crossed the mountains from Argentina to Chile, where the army became an important factor in the wars of liberation in Chile and Peru.

The end of Spanish rule in La Plata was less bloody but just as politically complicated as the wars of liberation in the rest of Spanish America. An officer named Francisco Javier de Elío, the commander of Montevideo, obtained recognition from the junta in Spain. Elío declared himself to be viceroy and prepared to attack Buenos Aires, where the criollos (people who were Spanish but born in the American colonies) had taken control and declared independence. An uprising in the interior of Banda Oriental (Uruguay) under the leadership of José Gervasio Artigas emerged. This commander offered his support to Buenos Aires, which was accepted. Artigas and Argentine troops invaded Banda Oriental, defeating the Spanish forces in May 1811. The only way Elío could save Montevideo was to call in Portuguese troops. A treaty in late 1811 was signed, and all parties agreed to withdraw their troops.[14]

Elío returned to Spain, where he became an important figure in restoring the Spanish monarchy as Napoleon's empire crumbled.

Buenos Aires, for all intents and purposes, had become independent. One question that took decades to resolve was the character of the new nation: was it to be a federation of provinces, or was it to be ruled from the capital? The *porteños*, as the people from the city and province of Buenos Aires were called, vied with the *provincianos*, people who hailed from the interior provinces; it was a classic case of conflict between the urban center and the rural periphery. The city dominated trade, but the provinces had a ready supply of formidable cavalrymen, who were recruited from the frontier cowboys called gauchos. The city had the advantage of considerable income from taxes on imports and exports.

A second question concerned the geographical extent of the new Argentine nation. Buenos Aires claimed all the land that had been subject to the Viceroyalty of La Plata, including Paraguay. Buenos Aires sent Colonel José de Espínola with a small force to Asunción, Paraguay's capital. He was arrogant and imperious and was heartily

---

[14] Hudson, Rex and Meditz, Sandra. *Uruguay: A Country Study.* Washington, DC, 1990. Library of Congress.

hated by the Paraguayans, who drove him out. In 1810, the Buenos Aires government sent General Manuel Belgrano, who was at the head of 1,500 cavalrymen, into Paraguay to take it over. In January 1811, Belgrano's cavalry collided with about six thousand Paraguayan militia and suffered a sharp defeat. He was driven back into Argentina.[15]

Buenos Aires called an assembly in 1813. Paraguay and Banda Oriental were invited, but Buenos Aires assumed that both would be provinces of Argentina. The assembly did not unify the old Viceroyalty of La Plata. Instead, Buenos Aires pushed for a single strong central government to be ruled from the city, while several of the provinces insisted on a loose federation. This dispute wracked Argentina for decades, sometimes descending into violent rebellion and war.

Artigas took power in Montevideo in a complicated series of conflicts. The issue in Montevideo was the same as in Argentina on a smaller scale (whether the government should be a strong central government or a loose assemblage of provinces). In 1816, the Portuguese again sent in several thousand troops. They eventually ousted Artigas, who found refuge in Paraguay.

On the other side of the Plata estuary, Brazil's experience in ending Portuguese rule was far different and far less violent than in the Spanish colonies. In 1807, the entire Portuguese court was faced with the advancing French Imperial Army. The Portuguese elite boarded British ships and sailed to Rio de Janeiro in Brazil, which became the de facto center of the Portuguese Empire. Portugal technically had a queen, Maria I, known as Maria the Mad. Her son, João (John), was regent, and he made all the decisions. He became King João VI upon her death. João VI declared Portugal and Brazil as equally important parts of the kingdom.

In 1816, the court sailed back to Portugal. Apparently, the king did so regretfully, preferring the relaxed life of the tropics to the cold formality of Lisbon. He left his son, Pedro, behind in Brazil as a kind of viceroy, and a series of political events in Portugal led to

---

[15] Whigham, Thomas. *The Paraguayan War: Causes and Early Conduct*, 2nd Edition. Calgary, Alberta: University of Calgary Press, 2018, 29-31.

independence being declared in 1822. Brazil emerged as the Empire of Brazil, with King João's son, Dom Pedro I, as the first emperor of Brazil.

Brazil retained the ancient Portuguese claims to Uruguay and Paraguay. The cattle ranches developing in Rio Grande do Sul were quickly expanding into Uruguay while ranchers from Argentina were migrating into Uruguay, setting up a conflict between Brazil and Argentina over the territory. This rivalry was central to the tensions that eventually resulted in the Paraguayan War.

Another major difference between the nations involved in the war is that the political form we know the nations as now in the 21st century did not exist then. For example, Brazil was under the rule of a constitutional monarch, Pedro I, who was then followed by his son, Brazilian-born Emperor Pedro II (1825–1891, r. 1831–1889), commonly known as Dom Pedro II. The movers and shakers in the Brazilian Empire were often rewarded with noble titles. For example, Luís Alves de Lima e Silva (1803–1880), the most successful Brazilian general of the Paraguayan War, was a victorious commander in other conflicts and was awarded the title of duke of Caxias. This fine soldier is known in history by the name of Caxias, his aristocratic title, rather than by his given name. Many other major figures in Brazilian history were made nobles and are known by their title rather than their surnames. Brazil remained formally the Empire of Brazil under Dom Pedro II until he was ousted in a military coup in 1889.

In 1860, Argentina was centered on the city and province of Buenos Aires but was wracked by disputes, rebellions, and civil wars between Buenos Aires and the interior provinces. These sometimes violent conflicts between centrists and those who wanted a loose federation of provinces were common in many nations in Latin America during the early years after independence. It took generations to resolve this conflict, which became particularly acute in the Argentine lands. This led to the rise of powerful regional leaders, mostly military or militia leaders, called *caudillos*. In Argentina, Buenos Aires was sometimes in control, and sometimes, the provinces united and formed what was essentially an independent nation.

Argentina in 1860 was not the huge nation it is today. It did not yet control all the Pampas or Patagonia. A sizable area of the interior plains in Argentina, the Pampas, was controlled by a federation of indigenous peoples under a Mapuche chief named Calfucurá (c. 1778–1873), who had crossed over the mountains from Chile and formed an extremely formidable tribal confederacy. In 1872, indigenous chiefs led six thousand warriors to attack interior cities and towns. The Argentine Army only ended native control in the interior in a series of hard-fought campaigns between 1879 and 1884.

Uruguay was still in the process of forming; it was not completely independent of either Brazil or Argentina, as was the case in Paraguay. Paraguay's deep history of near independence under the Jesuits during the Spanish colonial era seems to have given Paraguay a better sense of being different. The right of both Paraguay and Uruguay to exist as separate nations was threatened by the ambitions of Brazil and Argentina.

Chapter 4 – Dr. José Gaspar de Francia, *El Supremo*

Almost from independence to the end of the Paraguayan War, the country was ruled by three successive dictators. Each of the three rulers was unique and, in some ways, quite similar to the *caudillos* in Uruguay and the Argentine provinces. However, the *caudillos* were mostly men whose leadership grew from ranching and war. The three Paraguayan dictators were more urban, better educated, and every bit as ruthless.

One of the most unique dictators in history ruled Paraguay for a generation, from 1814 to 1840. Dr. José Gaspar Rodríguez de Francia proudly had the title of "doctor." His degree was a doctorate in theology from Argentina's University of Córdoba, which he was awarded in 1785. Dr. Francia (1766-1840) became a teacher at a religious school in Asunción, but his views were too advanced for the administration, so he began an alternate and more successful career as a lawyer.

Francia was very widely read, which was most unusual for a person from a remote city in the interior. He had enough money to support his leisure time reading. He is said to have learned four languages: Spanish, French, Guaraní, and some English. His father seems to have been an immigrant from Brazil, so Francia might have known a little Portuguese as well. He is also said to have learned enough Latin to read some of the classics in their original language. Guaraní was the predominant language spoken in Paraguay. It was originally an indigenous language but was heavily influenced by Spanish. Most of the few educated people in Asunción would have been bilingual in Spanish and Guaraní.

Francia read books by many of the authors of the French Enlightenment, apparently including Voltaire and Rousseau. Such books were viewed by the Spanish authorities with deep suspicion, and it is not known how Francia got his hands on them. They probably came via Buenos Aires, which, even in the early 1800s, was part of the world market. Books were among the contraband smuggled into the viceroyalty.

Francia's Brazilian ancestry was a problem in Paraguay. Brazilians were derided by the Creole elite as being descended from slaves, and there was a rumor that Francia was a mulatto, a person of mixed African and European ancestry. The biggest consequence of the rumor is that it prevented Francia from marrying the woman he loved because her family would not permit it based on his alleged African ancestry.[16]

The marriage that did not occur may be related to the law Francia enforced when he came to power, which forbade European Spaniards from marrying each other and only permitted them to marry mestizos, natives, or mixed-race people. It may also have helped create Francia's stern aura and his tendency to self-isolate.

Francia came to power in a complicated series of events. His work as a lawyer gave him popular support in Asunción, and his quiet academic demeanor probably made other people underestimate his political ability. He achieved power when he was nearly fifty years old. He had never been a soldier or military officer, unlike most of the others who rose to power in the aftermath of the Spanish colonial collapse. Unlike many other tyrants, Francia lived to a ripe old age for his time, dying of natural causes.

He was not part of the group ruling Asunción during the time of the Spanish. He apparently gained a great deal of popularity among the poor for his legal work. The poor in Asunción are known to have

---

[16] Cooney, Jerry. "Paraguayan Independence and Dr. Francia." *Americas* 28 (4) April 1972. 413. JSTOR access June 28, 2023.

held learning in great respect, something that was perhaps inherited from the days when Jesuits ran the thirty missions. Francia appears to have been an effective public speaker. In 1808, he became a minor official, a magistrate.

When news of the revolution in Buenos Aires came, the Paraguayans formed a committee and elected a council, a junta, that featured several respected men. Francia was chosen to join them. The pro-Spanish residents had no influence. The influential figures broke into two groups, one of which wanted to join Argentina and the other which sought Paraguayan independence. The accounts of events are confusing, but the upshot is that several consuls were elected, one of them being Francia, who outmaneuvered his opponents. Francia quit as consul at least once but was asked to come back because he was so respected.

In 1813, Francia convened a congress, which elected him dictator for three years. In June 1816, he convened another congress, which elected him dictator for life. The concept was perhaps borrowed from the idea of the ancient Roman dictators, who were elected by the Roman Senate and given absolute power for a limited time to solve extraordinary problems. The congress that elected him probably did not have in mind the kind of tyranny that Dr. Francia set up, at least the first time he was elected dictator.

Francia's appearance was more like that of a severe schoolmaster than a soldier. He had no uniform but a chest full of medals, and he carried no sword. Francia had a library filled with a thousand books, which must have been a record for dictators at the time. He has been described as gaunt looking, a man who "habitually wore a heavy black coat, a tricorn hat and outsized silver shoe buckles."[17]

[17] Whigham, Thomas. *The Paraguayan War: Causes and Early Conduct*, 2nd Edition. Calgary, Alberta: University of Calgary Press, 2018, 36.

A painting of Dr. Francia.

This professor-like dictator can be regarded as the principal figure in preserving Paraguay's independence. He declared independence in 1813 and managed to keep Argentina and Brazil at bay. He was paternalistic in the extreme and apparently felt contempt for only some of his opponents. Despite Francia's deep reading of the Enlightenment philosophers, he was no egalitarian. During his rule, he was capricious, and opposing him in any way was extremely dangerous. Francia ordered executions freely, and there was no appeal process. He was probably less murderous than most dictators of the time and certainly used the hangman and firing squad far less than Francisco Solano López did. Despite all that, Francia was fiercely devoted to Paraguay and retained popularity among the common people until his death.

Francia was originally educated for the priesthood, but he came to hold a strong animosity toward the church. Why he turned against the church is not known, though it may be related to his extensive reading of French philosophy. That philosophy produced the approach to a religion called deism, which also characterized some of the North Americans who founded the United States.

During the *Franciata*—as Francia's period of rule is often called—Francia banned religious orders, forced the clergy to swear loyalty to him personally, closed the only seminary in the country, and abolished the rights of clergy to be tried before religious instead of secular courts. He intentionally broke the political power of the church. This does not seem to have affected his popularity among the intensely religious population, perhaps because he also confiscated church lands and redistributed them to landless peasants. He also abolished tithes, which would have been a popular move among the poor.

Francia was extremely intelligent and appeared to have become increasingly egotistical as his power grew and his dictatorship was secured. He also seems to have developed a streak of paranoia. Francia seems to have been a man of relatively simple tastes, and unlike many dictators, he was not interested in enriching himself or his family. He was interested in reforming Paraguay and imposed his views sometimes with notable brutality. Francia was wildly popular with the lower classes in the country and was widely considered to be honest and competent, even by his opposition.[18]

Dr. Francia was not usually called by his actual name, instead being referred to as *El Supremo* while he was alive and as *El Difunto*, the Deceased One, after his death. Reportedly, many Paraguayans refused to believe he had died. It is difficult to assess whether stories like this are real or fiction.

There is no doubt Francia used spies at all levels of Paraguayan society and did not hesitate to strike when he was angry. He does not seem to have been much of a womanizer, unlike later dictators, and is not known to have had any descendants. He had no family to enrich

---

[18] Hanratty, Dana and Meditz, Sandra. *Paraguay: A Country Study*. Washington, DC: Library of Congress, 1988.

and no desire to enrich friends, unlike his successors. When Francia died, he left far more money in the country's treasury than was there when he assumed power, which was yet another aspect of his dictatorship that was rare among tyrants. Francia left Paraguay at peace, solvent, and mildly prosperous.

One oddity is that the famous Scottish essayist, historian, and philosopher Thomas Carlyle (1795–1881) wrote a lengthy essay about Francia. His 1843 essay was titled simply *Dr. Francia*. Carlyle had no firsthand experience with the dictator or with Paraguay. His information seems to have come from newspaper accounts, other historians, and what news was available of events in South America. British traders dominated the markets in the Plata region, so his information from travelers and merchants was both current and accurate.

Carlyle's essay was written after Francia's death and was explicit that Francia used terror and spies to control the country. However, Carlyle found much to praise about the tyrant. He portrayed Paraguay as peaceful and free from the violence that was common to some other countries on the continent. Carlyle admitted that Solano López was a tyrant but argued that orderly tyranny was better than chaos. Perhaps Carlyle was interested in Dr. Francia as a kind of philosopher king because Francia would have read many of the same Greek classics and Enlightenment writers that Carlyle had read. They were staples in the schooling of educated men (and it was mostly men in those days). Carlyle compared Francia to Britain's own past dictator, Oliver Cromwell.[19]

Paraguay was vulnerable on all sides. Brazil was expanding into the interior and also expanding to the south. The Argentine provinces represented a threat to Paraguay from the south and west because Argentina saw the Paraguayan regions as properly belonging to it. Hostile natives in the Chaco to the west and northeast were still a threat from the north. Paraguayans widely thought of Francia as a kind of father figure and protector. He was something of a father figure for the poor, but when faced with even a hint of rebellion, he reacted with

[19] Collmer, Robert. "Carlyle, Francia and Their Critics." Studies in Scottish Literature 14 (1), 1979. 1-12..

ferocity and prompt executions, some of them notably savage. But he protected Paraguay, avoided entanglements with Brazil and Argentina, and did much to develop his mostly rural and illiterate nation.

Francia was enamored with some of the Enlightenment ideas and sought to turn Paraguay into his version of an ideal state. Francia closed the borders, attempting to prevent people from entering or leaving the country. Thus, Paraguay became a kind of hermit country, something like North Korea today. It was not complete isolation because Francia welcomed Europeans who had expertise and provided sanctuary for a number of political figures fleeing persecution in neighboring countries. A problem for foreigners entering Paraguay was that Francia usually required that they remain in the country for the rest of their lives. Sealing off the borders had a drastic impact on Paraguay's exports of timber, hides, tobacco, and yerba mate, which declined to near zero.[20]

Francia famously detained the eminent French botanist Aimé Bonpland, a close associate of the world-famous scientist and philosopher Alexander von Humboldt. Bonpland had accompanied Humboldt in his epic 1799–1804 scientific expedition to the Americas and returned to France. He later decided to settle in Paraguay and made the mistake of trying to grow yerba mate commercially, which competed with Francia's monopoly. Bonpland's attempt was quashed, and he was arrested. Francia did not have him executed, which is mildly surprising. Instead, Bonpland was detained in Paraguay from 1821 to 1829.

Francia also had a strong dislike for *peninsulares*, residents who were born in Spain. In 1821, he had the three hundred or so of them in the country rounded up. Francia accused them of treason and imprisoned them for more than a year. He had them released when the group promised to pay 150,000 pesos, a huge sum for the time, equivalent to more than a year of the Paraguayan government's income. This forced payment broke their power in the economy. Many left or were exiled.[21]

---

[20] Hanratty, Dana and Meditz, Sandra. *Paraguay: A Country Study.* Washington, DC: Library of Congress, 1988.

[21] Ibid.

Stories about Francia abound. One of them that may or may not be true is that he was so frugal that he thought executing opponents by shooting them was a waste of good bullets, so he had executions done by bayonet instead. Another story that seems to be probably true is that Francia had a telescope, which he used to view the stars at night. Peering through a telescope at the night sky led some of the uneducated poor to think Francia was a wizard, capable of speaking with and controlling demons. Francia is also said to have used his telescope to make sure that streets were straight when he had sections of Asunción rebuilt.

Yet another story is that he did not have any advisors or trust anyone enough to be in that position but did use his barber as a sounding board for ideas and thoughts. Francia also had bouts of what was apparently hypochondria, and he would shut himself up for days on end, leaving Paraguay to govern itself.[22]

Dr. Francia was not a dictator in the usual Latin American *caudillo* style. He was not a man comfortable on horseback, and he had little experience in the gaucho lifestyle that was common to Juan Manuel de Rosas (dictator of Argentina) and elsewhere in the region. The only horse Francia regularly rode was the chair in his large personal library, and his rule was more a dictatorship by a professor than by a cowboy. It was nonetheless just as brutal and just as ruthless as the others.

There may or may not have been some conspiracies against him. Several were found in the years between 1817 and 1821. In 1820, a priest betrayed a confessional to report what may have been a plot, and in 1821, postal workers found evidence of a plot in a letter. It was said that postal surveillance was so ubiquitous that Paraguayans didn't bother to seal their letters. Francia ordered many of the suspects in various alleged plots to be executed. How many were actual conspirators and how many were simply accused by suspects under duress is not known.

Anyone who was accused faced terrible punishments. Francia had a place where suspects were regularly tortured. One standard treatment was to deliver one hundred to two hundred lashes with a

---

[22] Kennedy, Thomas. *Jose Gaspar Rodriguez de Francia and Francisco Solano López, as Historical Heroes.* Thesis, Texas Tech University, 1974, 36-37.

whip and then starve the suspect until they decided to tell their torturers what they wanted to hear. The place was known as the "Chamber of Truth."[23]

Late in his life, Francia developed a major paranoia about being assassinated. He slept in a different place every night for fear of being murdered in his sleep. He is also said to have prepared his own yerba mate and some of his food himself as a precaution against poisoning. Francia died from natural causes in 1840 at the age of seventy-four, with both the cause of death and his age being rather unusual for a dictator. One possible thing about Francia's death was quite unusual. There is a story that after he died, his body was fed to a caiman, a relative of the alligator.[24]

---

[23] Ibid, pgs. 27-28.

[24] War of the Triple Alliance. Com. "War of the Triple Alliance." Retrieved January 13, 2023.

Chapter 5 – Carlos Antonio López, *El Excelentisimo*

Following *El Supremo* Francia's death in 1840, some of his commanders contested with each other over who would take power. The possibility of a real republic or democracy seems to have been remote. There was a Paraguayan Congress under Francia, which continued to exist but had been reduced to a rubber stamp body. Congress was divided into factions, and for a time, politics was chaotic.

The man who managed to replace Francia was Carlos Antonio López (1787-1860), who established the López family as the controlling entity in Paraguay from 1844 to 1870. Like Francia, López became a dictator rather late in life, in his late fifties. He was an intelligent and educated man; he would have been one of the few educated people in the country. It's possible that some kind of residual respect for a university education helped López achieve power. There is nothing in López's history that suggests he would follow Francia as ruler.

Carlos Antonio was part of a triumvirate that took control of the government in 1841. He was designated one of three consuls, and like Francia, he managed to outmaneuver his competitors, quickly solidifying his control of the country. In 1844, Congress appointed him as president and did so several more times.

López was born in Asunción to a Spanish and indigenous family. López studied at the city's San Carlos Seminary and then taught there until Francia closed it. López married Juana Pabla Carrillo in 1826. He seems to have spent some of Francia's rule quietly away from Asunción on his wife's family ranch. Despite some prominence, López never attracted the ire of Dr. Francia and was never arrested or suspected of opposition.

López does not appear to have any characteristics that might have identified him as the next dictator. After Francia's death on September 20th, 1840, a junta (a group seizing power, usually a kind of military committee) was formed, but it fell apart in January 1841. It was followed by another junta, but this and others were ineffectual. López charmed his way to power. The Paraguayan Congress named López "First Consul," a highly significant term because it was the title Napoleon Bonaparte first used before he seized complete power.

Carlos Antonio differed from Dr. Francia in a number of ways. Unlike the austere Francia, he enjoyed what life had to offer and had no qualms about indulging himself. One of his indulgences was food. López became so enormously fat that near the end of his rule, he could no longer mount a horse and had to be driven in a carriage. He also was a notorious womanizer, and stories have it that he did not take rejection well. He also had a family (at least three sons and two daughters), and enriching his household was one of his main activities, unlike the incorruptible Francia. Like Francia, López was known by an informal but pervasive nickname, *El Excelentisimo*, the Most Excellent One. His ego more than matched Francia's, and he also became something of an egomaniac. López was not tolerant of criticism of his policies, family, or person.

Some of the actions that López took were every bit as unconventional as Dr. Francia's. López tried to prohibit the use of Guaraní last names because they sounded too native and too backward. His success in this project is not known, but it does indicate that he saw the indigenous Guaraní as somewhat backward. Carlos Antonio wanted Paraguay to be respected as modern and worked to make that happen. He opened Paraguay's borders to travelers.

López did much to develop Paraguay, including building palaces and impressive public buildings. This sometimes resulted in an impressive government building in a village that was otherwise a collection of shacks and hovels. López also built more useful infrastructure, including one of the first railways in South America and an armory capable of casting cannons. However, the few roads there were remained primitive, and the railroad was short and useful more for bragging rights than transportation. The steamboats López bought and had built at the armory were far more useful.

One important thing López did was to try to remedy illiteracy in Paraguay. Dr. Francia's priorities did not seem to have included schools. When Carlos Antonio began to take power in 1841, the country had one primary school. López built more than four hundred schools and sent promising Paraguayan students abroad to study. The country's population grew from about 200,000 to more than 400,000 during his years in power, and the country attained mild prosperity.[25]

There was some slavery in Paraguay, with some of the slaves owned by the state; they came from Francia's confiscations of property that he had forced on the elites as he destroyed their power. López did not abolish slavery, but he had Congress pass the Law of the Free Womb, which declared that any child of a Paraguayan slave would be free at the age of twenty-five. The law also abolished the slave trade but did not actually free the remaining adult slaves.

Under Francia, Paraguay was careful not to alienate either Brazil or Argentina, both of which were far more powerful than Paraguay. López was much less cautious, and in 1845, he declared war on Buenos Aires in support of a rebellion in the province of Corrientes, which borders Paraguay to the south. The rebellion was not successful, and there was not much actual fighting between Paraguay and Argentina. The city and province of Buenos Aires were ruled from 1835 to 1852 by the *caudillo* Juan Manuel de Rosas (1793–1877), who imposed an embargo on Paraguayan trade. When Rosas fell from power in 1852, López signed a treaty with the dominant Argentine faction; the treaty recognized Paraguayan independence.[26]

López not only built up the Paraguayan Army. In the 1840s, he also began to develop a navy, and in 1856, he began to erect an

[25] Hanratty, Dana and Meditz, Sandra. *Paraguay: A Country Study.* Washington, DC: Library of Congress, 1988.

[26] Ibid.

arsenal in Asunción that would also build steamships. It eventually built several of them but not from scratch. Some of the necessary equipment had to be imported from Britain, as did the engineers. The armory was successful but was not developed enough by the time the war began to manufacture any large quantities of weaponry. It was able to manufacture cannons, though.

The need for a naval presence was made plain by two incidents. In 1855, a US warship, the *Water Witch*, was on assignment, mapping surveys of the Paraná River system, when it was fired on by a Paraguayan fort, killing a sailor. At the time, the US protested but did not act until several years later. In February of 1859, the US sent a naval squadron to the La Plata River. Two warships steamed upriver to Asunción, the *Water Witch* and the *Fulton*. The American negotiator aboard obtained an apology for the incident, a $10,000 indemnity for the family of the sailor who had been killed in the 1855 incident, and a favorable treaty. In the second incident, which also took place in 1855, the Brazilians sent a fleet of twenty warships up the Paraguay River to warn the Paraguayans to stop interfering with Brazilian merchant shipping on the river route leading to Mato Grosso.[27]

A potentially much more serious incident occurred in 1859 when two British gunboats fired on the Paraguayan warship *Tacuarí* and temporarily captured it. The British were disputing several issues with Paraguay and had banned Paraguayan naval vessels from steaming outside the Paraná system. The *Tacuarí* was sailing from Buenos Aires to Montevideo, apparently in some kind of attempt at mediating one of the political disputes in Uruguay. On board was Francisco Solano López, who had recently been appointed a general, and Paraguay's minister of war.[28]

López turned some of Paraguay's assets into monopolies, which was how he financed his palaces and other projects. He turned the export of yerba mate into a monopoly and did the same with timber. Congress enacted a conscription law for all able-bodied men, which

[27] Ehlers, Hartmut. "The Paraguayan Navy, Past and Present." *Warship International* 41 (1), 2004. 80. JSTOR access, January 12, 2023.

[28] Ibid, pg. 81.

provided unpaid labor for various state projects. This kind of conscription does not seem to have caused opposition and set the pattern for conscription in the coming war.[29]

López developed a relationship with the London firm of J. & A. Blyth. The Blyth firm recruited dozens of engineers and technical experts for the various infrastructure projects in Paraguay. Most of the experts were British, and several left accounts of their experiences, which have proven useful for historians. They appear to have been well paid. Some of them remained in Paraguay during the war, and several paid for that with their lives,

The relationship between Carlos Antonio and his son is not particularly well known. He appointed his son as brigadier general while he was a teenager, which suggests either confidence or fatherly doting. Francisco Solano was intelligent and apparently a good student, at least in things in which he was interested, like fortifications and artillery. Carlos Antonio made sure that his son was educated, and he had enough confidence in his son to send him to Europe with broad authority to sign contracts and make deals.

Carlos Antonio was a dictator, not simply a figure linking the regimes of two of the most infamous tyrants in South American history. In retrospect, his regime seems mild and even beneficial.

[29] Whigham, Thomas. *The Paraguayan War: Causes and Early Conduct*, 2nd Edition. Calgary, Alberta: University of Calgary Press, 2018, 64-70.

Chapter 6 – Francisco Solano López, *El Mariscal*

Francisco Solano López was born in 1827. Or maybe 1826. There is one story that his birthdate was fudged so that he would be considered a legitimate son of Carlos Antonio. The story may or may not be true, but anyone spreading it during the lifetimes of the López dictators would probably have shortened their own lifetime.

The younger López was appointed brigadier general in 1844 when he was eighteen. He saw service in the skirmishes with Argentine strongman Rosas, and he studied military history. Just what kind of military matters he studied or where is unclear. This is just one of a number of aspects of López that are reported differently in biographical materials. One reports he studied in Rio de Janeiro, which seems unlikely given his dislike for Brazilians. Another claims he studied at the famed St. Cyr in France. There is no doubt, however, that he was an observer of the Allied armies in Crimea during the Crimean War.

The critical part of his military education came in 1853 when Carlos Antonio appointed his son as a kind of roving diplomat with a special mission to purchase weaponry for Paraguay and probably to learn some social polish in France. Francisco Solano visited several countries and was an observer of the bloody Crimean War (1853–1856). In that war, an alliance of British, French, Ottoman Turks, and Sardinians fought Russians in Crimea in the Black Sea. The formidable Russian fortress of Sevastopol resisted an Allied siege for far longer than expected, and Francisco Solano seems to have absorbed the lesson. He later greatly strengthened the Paraguayan fortress complex at Humaitá, which also resisted an Allied siege far longer than expected.[30]

Francisco Solano stayed in Paris much of the time he was in Europe and came to admire another dictator, Emperor Napoleon III of France. The culture of Napoleon's court is sometimes called the Second Empire, and it was consciously modeled on that of Napoleon I in an attempt to make the sometimes-bumbling Napoleon III seem more like an emperor. In a way, it was reflected glory, but Napoleon III was a real autocrat nonetheless. The emperor controlled France like the autocrat he was and led the country into military adventures designed to create glory for himself and France. López found the military uniforms and the constant reminders of past glory to be quite congenial. He took a liking to French uniforms and the French Army and brought ideas from them back to Paraguay.

Francisco Solano was invited to the French court, perhaps as a curiosity or perhaps as a strategy to advance French interests. He would have been impressed with the court of Empress Eugénie de Montijo, a Spanish beauty (1826–1920). He may have met Eliza Lynch there. This chance meeting with a well-connected Irish courtesan proved to be important to his life and the history of Paraguay.

López's is irrevocably mixed in with the story of his romance with his mistress, Irish-born Eliza Alice Lynch (1833–1886). They never married, but they had six children together, including five sons. López, like his father, was a compulsive womanizer, but he remained steadily attached to Eliza until he was shot down. They remained together despite his frequent affairs. That means they were together for sixteen or seventeen years until a time when Lynch would have been seen as middle-aged.

Eliza Lynch was born in Ireland in 1833, but her family relocated

---

[30] Redington, Erick. "The Paraguayan President Who Brought His Country to Military Catastrophe." *History is Now Magazine* online. Parts 1, 2, 3 and 4. Retrieved January 13, 2023.

to France to the household of Eliza's uncle after the death of her father in 1846. When she was sixteen, she married Xavier Quatrefages, a French Army officer who was stationed in Algeria. One biographer claims that she was tricked into marrying him. He was considerably older, and for some unknown reason, the marriage did not work out. She left her husband in Algeria and fled to Paris to join her mother.[31]

Another story has it that Eliza was set up or set herself up as a courtesan, but the evidence is unclear whether she was a high society prostitute or a gold digger (or perhaps something both). She seems to have had influential friends. In Paris, she somehow came to the attention or got herself introduced to the dashing young son of a South American dictator named Francisco Solano López. The young López was also an army officer, and perhaps Eliza found that attractive. López knew Spanish and French, but whether he knew much English is questionable. Eliza would have been fluent in French, so perhaps they conversed with each other in that language. López appears to have had a talent for languages because he was also fluent in Guaraní and may have known some Portuguese.

The young López was smitten with Eliza, and she appears to have really fallen for him rather than seeing him as just a meal ticket. She sailed for Paraguay in 1855, where López was waiting for her. Eliza was welcomed and appeared to have added a Parisian touch to ceremonies and social events in Asunción. Historians do not have any consistent interpretation of Eliza. For almost a decade, she was the consort of the dictator-heir apparent and then first lady of the dictator. Some see her as a 19th-century version of Argentina's Evita Perón, and others see her as a grasping consort who turned López into a brutal tyrant. Today, she is regarded in Paraguay as a hero.[32]

---

[31] Lillis, Michael. "The True Origins of Eliza Lynch." *The Irish Times*, March 11, 2014.

[32] Ibid.

A picture of Eliza from around 1855.
https://commons.wikimedia.org/wiki/File:Eliza_lynch_1855.jpg

Francisco Solano and his Irish paramour were dominant in the social scene in Asunción. What his dictator father thought of Lynch is not known, but as the mother of five sons, she had a certain status in a highly paternalistic culture. What the other families in Asunción thought about a former French courtesan achieving the limelight in their city is not known either, but they kept their criticism to themselves for obvious reasons.

When Carlos Antonio died, his son was in the building. Francisco Solano immediately took control of his father's papers and will. He was already vice president of the country, and the will designated him as his father's successor. As vice president, he could call a session of Congress and did so. Francisco Solano had the building where they met surrounded by soldiers, ostensibly for security. It surprised no one when he was named president of Paraguay. Congress awarded him a lavish sword, designated him as field marshal of Paraguay, and, interestingly, passed a law prohibiting López from risking his life in battle.[33]

López did not need anyone to turn him into a tyrant; that seems to have come naturally to him and may have been learned from his father, who was an expert in matters of tyranny. The senior López had been interested in enriching his family, and the younger López seems to have been interested in enriching Eliza. López kept turning state properties over to her. By 1864, she may have owned more property than any other woman in the world, owning property said to be one and a half times the size of Ireland.[34]

There is no consensus among historians about the younger López. Some see him as a paranoid megalomaniac. Others see him as a murderous beast or a small-scale Stalin. Still, others see him as the heroic leader of a small nation fighting for its existence. It is unclear if he had the same concerns as Carlos Antonio, of enriching himself and yet also developing Paraguay. Francisco Solano's peacetime rule was too short to make a meaningful comparison with the much longer rule of his father.

Because of López's experiences in Europe, he may have known as much about military affairs as anyone in Paraguay. However, when it came to choosing officers, he appears to have considered personal loyalty as the most important trait. As a result, during the Paraguayan War, some of the Paraguayan commanders were incompetent. In a way, this paralleled the Brazilian tendency to appoint officers based on their social position rather than their military competency.

López had an efficient propaganda apparatus. The content of newspapers was carefully controlled, and stories that presented López as an all-powerful and supremely competent leader were constant. Dissent was highly dangerous and seemingly rare. As was the case during the time of his father, even Communion in the churches was compromised, with priests strongly encouraged to report seditious

[33] Kennedy, Thomas. *Jose Gaspar Rodriguez de Francia and Francisco Solano López, as Historical Heroes.* Thesis, Texas Tech University, 1974, 51.

[34] Lillis, Michael. "The True Origins of Eliza Lynch." *The Irish Times,* March 11, 2014.

thoughts or comments.[35]

Asunción had a newspaper, *El Semanario,* and it was a ceaseless voice for López. In 1868, a certain padre (priest) named Maíz was released from prison and became some kind of writer for the paper. He consistently presented López as equivalent to Jesus, perhaps because he believed it or more likely because he had enough of prison.[36]

Paraguayans had experienced a police state beginning in 1814, so they were used to it. The problem with Francisco Solano López is that he might have believed his regime's propaganda. He had grown up as the son and heir apparent to Carlos Antonio and, unlike his father, had never had to be careful about offending the ruler. Carlos Antonio had to be careful not to offend Dr. Francia because offending Francia could have cost him his life. Francisco Solano had no such chastening experiences.

In Francisco Solano's last years during the war, he did emerge as a murderous tyrant. He had his two brothers and two brothers-in-law executed because he suspected them of disloyalty and defeatism. He had some five hundred foreigners executed, apparently having them killed by bayonet and machete to save ammunition. He is also said to have tortured his mother and sisters because he thought they were disloyal, and he is also said to have ordered thousands of executions of Paraguayans during the war. He apparently was about to have US Ambassador Charles Washburn executed, but Washburn was saved by the appearance of the USS *Wasp,* a US Navy gunboat.[37]

Desertion and cowardice were apt to result in execution, and López had some officers executed, interpreting their lack of success as cowardice or failure to properly carry out orders. In the last months of the war, boys as young as ten were drafted into the army, and soldiers went into battle barefoot. Much of the nearly psychotic mayhem

---

[35] Redington, Erick. "The Paraguayan President Who Brought His Country to Military Catastrophe." *History is Now Magazine* online 1, 2, 3 and 4. Retrieved January 13, 2023.

[36] Kennedy, Thomas. *Jose Gaspar Rodriguez de Francia and Francisco Solano López, as Historical Heroes.* Thesis, Texas Tech University, 1974, 55.

[37] Hanratty, Dana and Meditz, Sandra. *Paraguay: A Country Study.* Washington, DC: Library of Congress, 1988.

López has been accused of appears to have been factual.

Allied propaganda portrayed him as a murderous and uncivilized tyrant. It is also evident that his orders to "conquer or die" were sometimes followed out of fear of the consequences, but many Paraguayans continued to offer determined resistance long after they could have safely deserted or gone over to the enemy. Fear of López certainly motivated Paraguayan fighters, but so did hatred of the Brazilians and the fear for Paraguay's future. It cannot be determined whether fear of López or patriotism or both caused the fierce Paraguayan resistance that prolonged the war.

A picture of Francisco Solano, c. 1870.
https://commons.wikimedia.org/wiki/File:Francisco_Solano_Lopez_Carrillo.jpg

Chapter 7 – Trouble in Gaucho Country

The country now called Uruguay has a history that has been closely linked to Paraguay. Part of the reason is that Montevideo, Uruguay's capital, was a port and that Paraguayan access to either Buenos Aires or Montevideo required free navigation of the Paraguay, Paraná, and La Plata rivers. Part of the relationship between the two countries is that both were in the contested regions between the Spanish and Portuguese colonial empires.

Uruguay was often called Banda Oriental, meaning the east bank of the Plata estuary. Environmentally, it was much like the adjacent regions of Argentina but was split by the wide estuary. From the Brazilian point of view, it was the Cisplatine province on their side of the Plata estuary.

Spanish loyalists gave up on preserving Spanish authority in Uruguay in 1814. They had been expelled by the forces of a local *caudillo* named José Gervasio Artigas (1764-1850). The Portuguese had a lively interest in annexing the area after Spanish authority collapsed, and Buenos Aires assumed that it would become a part of Argentina. Artigas was also something of a populist and welcomed a wide range of groups into his movement, apparently treating them all equally. He recruited free people of color, natives, poor Creoles, and *castas* (people of mixed race). The support Artigas got from the poor and downtrodden alarmed the middle class and wealthy in the cities, so they backed other *caudillos* who were less obviously radical.[38]

Artigas tried to ensure an independent Uruguay or, as people often called it then, Banda Oriental. He was defeated by the Portuguese in 1817. Artigas continued to be an influential figure in Uruguay for a time but sought refuge in Paraguay and died in Asunción in 1850 as a guest of Carlos Antonio.

Like Paraguay, Uruguay had been lightly populated during the Spanish colonial era, but most of the inhabitants spoke Spanish and were not receptive to the Portuguese. Some Uruguayans who resisted the Brazilian occupation fled to Argentina and eventually obtained support for their goal of eliminating Brazilian control. The Argentines were still fragmented, and an alliance called the United Provinces decided to aid the Uruguayans.

A rather sanguine war broke out between Argentina, Brazil, and Uruguayan rebels. The Cisplatine War lasted from 1825 to 1828. "Cisplatine" was a name used by Brazil to refer to Uruguay in the sense of "this side of the Plata." Brazil named it that way to assert its claim. The region was occupied by troops from Portuguese Brazil in 1816 and continued to be occupied by independent Brazil. Upon achieving independence, Brazilian Emperor Pedro I declared Uruguay to be a province of the Brazilian Empire, giving it the formal name "Cisplatine Province." The Uruguayans were not interested in being Brazilians, and both Argentina and Paraguay opposed Brazilian interests in Uruguay.

In April 1825, a group of Uruguayans crossed the Plata into Uruguay from Argentina. The group was led by Juan Antonio Lavalleja and had considerable support from the Argentines. They started a revolt that threatened to oust the Brazilian administration. In October 1825, the rebels met and defeated a small Brazilian force and declared Uruguay a province of Argentina. At that time, Argentina was more a loose federation than an organized entity and was known as the United Provinces of Rio de la Plata.[39]

---

[38] Whigham, Thomas. *The Paraguayan War: Causes and Early Conduct*, 2nd Edition. Calgary, Alberta: University of Calgary Press, 2018, 35-36.

[39] Global Security.Org. "Cisplatine War, 1825-28." globalsecurity.org/military/world/cisplatine/. Retrieved January 21, 2023.

Brazil had a small standing army and a rather powerful navy, so it blockaded Buenos Aires. The United Provinces did not have much of an army and even less of a navy but managed to put together a formidable army, mostly made up of the gaucho horsemen. The United Provinces even managed to form a small navy that seems to have acquitted itself rather well. The fighting on land came later in the war when the United Provinces and Uruguayans invaded Rio Grande do Sul. The culminating action was the battle on Ituzaingó in Rio Grande do Sul, which pitted seven thousand Uruguayan and United Provinces troops against about six thousand Brazilians. The Brazilians lost, and the defeat resulted in the loss of the Cisplatine province (Uruguay).

The British had a strong interest in ending the Cisplatine War because it was interfering with the growing trade from the La Plata River, which was heavily dominated by British interests. They offered to mediate, and the offer was accepted by both sides. The British suggested that Banda Oriental/Cisplatine become independent. Both sides agreed to withdraw their troops and await developments from the Uruguayans. Uruguay formed a government and adopted a constitution that both the Argentines and Brazilians found acceptable. In July 1830, Uruguay became an independent country under its first president, General José Fructuoso Rivera. Uruguay became independent but still remained a buffer zone between Argentina and Brazil, much as Paraguay was. The war ended, and for a time, the region became calm.[40]

However, tensions between the Argentines and Brazilians remained, and the Plata area as a whole remained subject to political instability. The people in Rio Grande do Sul—the *Riograndenses*— were themselves restive and chafed under the Brazilian government. There were a number of minor rebellions, at least one of which flared up into something larger, although Brazil quelled the rebellion. There was little danger the province would secede or attempt to join an Argentine federation.[41]

---

[40] Ibid.

[41] Whigham, Thomas. *The Paraguayan War: Causes and Early Conduct*, 2nd Edition. Calgary, Alberta: University of Calgary Press, 2018, 61.

Uruguay had no particular historical or cultural claim to a separate existence in the sense that the Jesuit missions to the Guaraní people had given to Paraguay. It shared cattle and ranching cultural characteristics of the adjacent areas, the Brazilian province of Rio Grande do Sul and the interior provinces of Argentina. What Uruguay did have was an apparently endless struggle between the Blancos and the Colorados, the main political parties, which sometimes broke into open warfare and frequently resulted in Argentine or Brazilian intervention.

Events in Uruguay continued to be unsettled. From 1843 to 1852, Uruguay underwent a civil war, later called the "Great War." Uruguay had two contesting governments. One was the Colorados, based in Montevideo, who wanted a strong central government, and then there were the Blancos, who were based in the provinces and sought a loose federation of provinces. Montevideo was under siege for years, supplied by sea from Buenos Aires. In 1851, Brazil intervened in favor of the Colorados. The Colorados agreed to a treaty that was highly favorable to Brazil. The treaty gave Brazil the right to intervene in Uruguayan political affairs, required that slaves escaping from Brazil be returned, and gave Brazil the rights of navigation on the Uruguay River, among other things.[42]

Argentine dictator Rosas controlled Buenos Aires until 1852. He meddled in Uruguay and antagonized Brazilian interests there by sending in troops in 1852. Brazil once again went to war with Buenos Aires, defeating Rosas at the Battle of Monte Caseros. Some five thousand Brazilian troops remained in Uruguay until 1855. By 1860, some twenty thousand Brazilians and their slaves had settled in Uruguay, mostly gauchos and cattle ranchers from Rio Grande do Sul. These Brazilian migrants constituted somewhere between 10 and 15 percent of the population and became an important part of the complicated political situation in Uruguay. They were not necessarily pro-Brazil because some had fled Brazil rather than seek unoccupied land. They were Brazilian, though, and spoke Portuguese.[43]

[42] Hudson, Rex and Meditz, Sandra. *Uruguay: A Country Study.* Washington, DC, 1990. Library of Congress.

[43] Bethell, Leslie. "The Paraguayan War 1864-70." Page 95 in Leslie Bethell, *Brazil: Essays on*

López's decision to declare war in 1865 caused more trouble between the Blancos and the Colorados in Uruguay. The history of the two parties was one of ancient detestation that seems to have been as real as their actual political differences.

The Blancos, who were conservatives, were in power in Montevideo in 1863 when a gaucho general, Venancio Flores, raised yet another rebellion with the backing of the Colorados, who were liberals. Flores repeatedly crossed into Uruguay with Brazilian backing with the intent to topple the Blancos and their government. Uruguayan troops chased his raiders back into Brazilian territory and caused damage, for which the Brazilian government demanded payment.

The Blancos appealed to Paraguay for help, and López decided to intervene. López seems to have heartily detested the Brazilians and was also worried that they might seize Uruguay and block Paraguay's access to the sea. With the aid of Brazil, General Flores and his Colorados ousted the Uruguayan president and took control of the country. López decided to send his army into Uruguay and requested that he be allowed to cross Argentine territory to reach Uruguay. Permission was refused, and the powder keg was ignited.

History and Politics. London: University of London Press, 2018.

Chapter 8 – Solano López invades Argentina and Brazil

The Blanco government sought help from Paraguay, and López offered to mediate the issue. Brazil refused mediation, and on August 30th, 1864, López issued an ultimatum that stated sending Brazilian troops into Uruguay would be considered an act of war. In October, Brazil blockaded Montevideo and landed troops in support of General Flores. This is the context of the Paraguayan seizure of the Brazilian ship *Marquês de Olinda* on November 12th, 1864, on the Río Paraguay.[44] As with other aspects of the war, the reported details vary. The Brazilian ship steamed to places in Mato Grosso once a month, and on this trip was the newly appointed governor of that province. The steamer was also carrying supplies of weapons and ammunition. One source says that the Brazilians provided the Paraguayans with a manifest of what was on board and that López sent a Paraguayan Navy steamer to intercept and bring her back to Asunción.[45]

---

[44] Abente, Diego. "The War of the Triple Alliance: Three Explanatory Models." *Latin American Research Review* 22 (2), 1987. 48. JSTOR access, January 12, 2023.

[45] Kennedy, Thomas. *Jose Gaspar Rodriguez de Francia and Francisco Solano López, as Historical Heroes.* Thesis, Texas Tech University, 1974, 45.

The crew and all on board were arrested. The new governor of Mato Grosso survived and was allowed to return to Brazil apparently because the US ambassador, Charles Washburn, intervened. All but one of the remaining crew and passengers died in custody. Brazil took the incident as an act of war. The steamer itself was unharmed and incorporated into the Paraguayan river navy.

López wanted to send his army to aid Uruguay. It is more than eight hundred miles from Asunción to Montevideo, so reaching anywhere in Uruguay would require the army to cross through the Argentine province of Corrientes or Misiones or through Rio Grande do Sul in Brazil. The two Argentine provinces jut out from northeast Argentina like a thumb, with an elongated shape roughly bearing southwest to northeast. Corrientes is the western province, and Misiones is the east. The two Argentine provinces have Paraguay to the north, Uruguay to the south and southeast, and Brazil's Rio Grande do Sul to the east.

In January 1865, López made the fateful request that Argentina should allow his army to cross Argentine territory to reach Uruguay. Argentina refused the request, and López decided to declare war on Argentina. The rubber-stamp Paraguayan Congress met on March 23rd and passed a declaration of war. They also promoted López to field marshal. The declaration of war reached Buenos Aires on March 29th.

Why López had the *Marquês de Olinda* seized is unclear. Any Brazilian ship on the river was, in effect, a potential hostage, and seizing a provincial governor was especially provocative and certain to start a conflict. López plainly knew that Brazil had a far larger population and a strong navy. The Paraguayans, at that time, had the largest army in South America. Perhaps López thought a swift attack would achieve his goals in Uruguay before Brazil could mobilize.

The conflict began with López declaring war. The war can be divided into three phases: the Paraguayan campaign in Mato Grosso and invasions of Argentine and Brazilian territory in 1864 and early 1865, the Allied invasion of Paraguay in 1866, and the guerrilla phase from 1869 to 1870 after the fortress of Humaitá fell, with Asunción falling shortly after. After the Allies' initial victories upon invading Paraguay, they experienced a stunning defeat, and the war was a bloody stalemate for many months.[46]

López's action was poorly timed. Paraguay had large orders of weapons in Europe paid for and ready to be shipped, but they could not be delivered because the Brazilians quickly set up a blockade. The weapons that never came included several batteries of advanced French field artillery, thirty-six pieces of Krupp heavy artillery, and two ironclad warships.[47]

It is unknown what effect these weapons would have had if Paraguay had actually received them. Paraguayan artillery in defensive fortifications was quite formidable, and the two ironclads might have effectively resisted Brazil's overwhelming naval force. As it happened, at least one of the ironclad warships the Paraguayans had ordered and partly paid for wound up in the Brazilian Navy and was used against Paraguay.

While the war began in December 1864 with the Paraguayan invasion of Mato Grosso, the Triple Alliance was not formed until May 1st, 1865. Venancio Flores triumphed in Uruguay with the help of Brazilian troops, and both Argentina and Brazil were already at war with López. A treaty was agreed to, and the Allies began to coordinate and join forces. The treaty specified that the war would not end until López was removed from power. A secret clause in the treaty dealt with border issues and specified that Paraguay would pay an indemnity and that Paraguay's national existence would not be threatened.

---

[46] Bethell, Leslie. "The Paraguayan War 1864-70." Page 100 in Leslie Bethell, *Brazil: Essays on History and Politics*. London: University of London Press, 2018.

[47] Ehlers, Hartmut. "The Paraguayan Navy, Past and Present." *Warship International* 41 (1), 2004. 96. JSTOR access, January 12, 2023.

The contested territories in 1864 in the La Plata region.

Although at the very start of the war, López had an army considerably bigger than the forces of all three of the Allies totaled, Paraguay's military potential was far smaller than that of the Triple Alliance. A measure of the disparity in resources is the total value of imports and exports in 1860. Paraguay's was £560,000; Argentina's was £8,950,000; Brazil's was £23,739,000; and Uruguay's was £3,600,000.[48]

---

[48] Abente, Diego. "The War of the Triple Alliance: Three Explanatory Models." *Latin American Research Review* 22 (2), 1987. 54. JSTOR access, January 12, 2023.

Despite the huge difference in population and resources, at the start of the war, Paraguay's army was, on paper, capable of the invasions López undertook. Estimates vary, but Paraguay had somewhere between sixty thousand and seventy-seven thousand men under arms, an enormous number considering the country's small population. Paraguay had already mobilized its army, which was aided by the fact that López had much of the army permanently mobilized as a workforce for public projects.

López may have expected to be supported by one or more of the provincial *caudillos* in Argentina. The city and province of Buenos Aires was the largest and most powerful Argentine entity, but the country did not yet have effective unity. Although the Paraguayans hoped for either the support or the active help of one or more of the provincial leaders, many of the leaders of the other provinces disliked the *porteños*. None of them sided with López.

López seems to have particularly hoped for the assistance of Justo José de Urquiza, the *caudillo* who controlled the Argentine provinces of Corrientes and Entre Ríos. Urquiza was often at odds with Buenos Aires, and López anticipated his active support because of that. This powerful *caudillo* led the forces of the interior provinces against Buenos Aires in an actual war in 1859, so López's hopes that the division among the Argentinians would lead to Urquiza being supportive or at least neutral was reasonable. However, Urquiza (1801–1870) sided with Buenos Aires during the war and provided troops against López. He was assassinated in 1870 because of Argentine politics rather than anything to do with his limited participation in the war.

Argentina's participation in the Paraguayan War was limited by the lack of unity among the provinces. At one point, President Bartolomé Mitre had to send troops back to Argentina to deal with a rebellion. However, López got neither the assistance nor the neutrality he seemed to have gambled on.

Argentine provinces were unruly and greatly affected the number of troops sent to the war. By 1869, most of the troops from Argentina were withdrawn from Paraguay to deal with disturbances at home. One count is that in the years from 1862 to 1868, Argentina experienced 117 rebellions of varying degrees of seriousness, and the rebels caused 91 actual battles, costing an estimated 5,000 deaths.[49]

Despite Paraguay's initial advantage of numbers, Brazil had by far the largest navy in the region and the largest in South America, including thirty-three steam-powered and twelve sail warships. The navy was well trained and had career professional officers. This meant that the Allies had control of the sea and much of the river system from the start of the war. They could transport large numbers of troops by water rather than marching overland through swamps and on very poor road systems. Brazil also had fairly good credit and, therefore, the ability to raise some loans in Europe to buy weapons. Brazil quickly placed orders for weapons and ships, and by 1865, several ironclads had arrived.[50]

[49] Penalta, Alfredo Fornos. "Draft Dodgers, War Resisters, and Turbulent Gauchos: The War of the Triple Alliance Against Paraguay." *Americas* 38 (4) April 1982. 472-73. JSTOR access January 28, 2023.

[50] Bethell, Leslie. "The Paraguayan War 1864-70." Page 95 in Leslie Bethell, *Brazil: Essays on History and Politics.* London: University of London Press, 2018.

Chapter 9 – The Mato Grosso Campaign

In December 1864, López decided to invade Brazil's Mato Grosso province, which bordered much of Paraguay to the north and northeast. He sent a force of several thousand men upriver, carried by the Paraguayan Navy, the flagship of which was the *Tacuarí*. This campaign was very difficult for the Brazilians to defend against because the province was remote, had a small population, and was really only accessible by the river. With Humaitá blocking the Paraguay River, Brazilian reinforcements could no longer travel upriver and could only reach the province by trekking overland, which was very slow and arduous.

For many years, Mato Grosso had been a bone of contention between Paraguay and Brazil, with the Brazilians insisting on their right to communicate with the province by using Paraguayan rivers. There were sporadic native raids across the unmarked border into Paraguay. In Portuguese days, natives had traded captured Paraguayan cattle to Portuguese settlers for guns and other goods, a tradition that continued. Paraguay suspected Brazilian connivance with the native raids.

In 1855, Carlos Antonio sent secret instructions to his commander on the northern border, ordering a retreat should the Brazilians attack from Mato Grosso. The Paraguayan forces were not to stand and fight but were to start a guerrilla war to "molest the enemy, wear him down and immobilize him."[51]

There had been little trouble from troops in Mato Grosso at that time, and Brazil had only small garrisons in the province in 1865, far too few to resist the Paraguayan expeditionary force.

The main Paraguayan force of about five thousand men was transported up the Paraguay River into Brazilian territory. The troops landed and besieged the small Brazilian fort at Nova Coimbra. They captured the fort after three days of stiff resistance. The remains of the Brazilian force were allowed to escape on a small gunboat. The Brazilian commander, Lieutenant colonel Portocarrero, was later ennobled by Dom Pedro II; he was given the title Baron Coimbra after the fort.[52]

A second and smaller Paraguayan force invaded Brazilian territory slightly to the south of Mato Grosso, where it defeated the few Brazilian forces stationed there and occupied some towns. One small Brazilian detachment was commanded by Lieutenant Antônio Ribeiro and was killed to the man. That resistance has since entered into Brazilian military legend.

The Paraguayans were accused of looting everything in sight and destroying what they could not send back to Asunción. Whether that was a conscious policy or not, the Paraguayan occupation caused a great deal of damage to the scantily populated province. Brazilian settlers fled, and the Paraguayans controlled much of Mato Grosso for several years, although chaos and anarchy characterized the region. Although the number of troops was relatively small, the death rate was high, primarily because of disease.

The most important result of the invasion was that Paraguay captured a substantial quantity of weapons, apparently enough to significantly assist the entire war effort for more than a year. The impact on Paraguayan morale was good, and the Brazilians were chagrined that Brazilian territory had been invaded and occupied.

---

[51] Williams, John. "The Undrawn Line: Three Centuries of Strife on the Paraguayan- Mato Grosso Border." *Luso-Brazilian Studies* 17 (1), Summer 1980. 31. JSTOR access January 24, 2023.

[52] Military History. "The Mato Grosso Campaign." military-history.fandom.comwiki/ Mato_Grosso_Campaign/. Retrieved January 24, 2023.

A Brazilian column of about three thousand infantry marched overland to Mato Grosso. Their march was another minor epic, covering well over a thousand miles and going through several Brazilian provinces. The number actually arriving in the province was under two because of disease and desertion. This force found several Paraguayan positions abandoned and managed to invade some miles into Paraguayan territory but were easily chased out. Much of the province remained under Paraguayan control for several years.

The Paraguayan invasion of Mato Grosso seems to have been a diversionary campaign, with the aim of distracting Brazilian attention and resources from the much more important campaigns in the south. The Paraguayan occupation of much of southern Mato Grosso lasted until April 1868, when the few remaining troops were pulled out when they were needed in the battles in southern Paraguay.[53]

The Mato Grosso campaign was the most successful Paraguayan campaign of the war. It did little in the way of diverting either Brazilian troops or resources, so its overall impact was small. It did disrupt the flow of what diamonds and gold were produced in the province and prevented Brazil from resupplying the province by the river.

Paraguay also quickly struck hard at Argentina and elsewhere in Brazil. On April 13th, the Paraguayan Navy and Army, in cooperation with a land invasion force of several thousand troops, took control of the Argentine river port of Corrientes, downriver from Humaitá, not far from where the Paraguay flows into the Paraná, on the eastern side of the river. They captured two Argentine warships in the process. After the occupation of the town of Corrientes, a Paraguayan force continued to advance down the Paraná. Farther east, a second Paraguayan column crossed the Uruguay River and advanced south into Brazilian territory, the northern part of the province of Rio Grande do Sul.

This second column was commanded by Colonel Antonio de la Cruz Estigarribia, and it was considerably stronger than the force that took Corrientes, numbering about twelve thousand men. The force was to march down the Uruguay River but on the river's south side,

---

[53] Ibid.

which was very much in Brazil. López may have wanted to use this attack as a diversion because it was too small a force to occupy much territory. The colonel's force continued to march down the river and captured the Brazilian river town of Uruguaiana on August 5th and stopped there.

The Paraguayan commander had earlier divided his forces, which was a serious mistake. A detachment of about three thousand Paraguayan infantry and cavalry that had no artillery collided with an Allied force led by Flores, the *caudillo* recently installed as president of Uruguay. Flores had united his troops with some from Brazil and Argentina, giving him some eight thousand men, including more than two dozen cannons. The Allies attacked and destroyed the Paraguayan forces at the Battle of Yatay on August 17th, 1865. An estimated 1,700 Paraguayans were killed, and 1,200 were captured. A few hundred swam across the river and escaped. The battle gravely weakened Estigarribia's army and essentially ended the possibility that the Paraguayans might turn south or east to raid deeper into Brazil.

The Brazilian Navy controlled the Uruguay River too. About eighteen thousand Allied troops from all three nations converged on the force in Uruguaiana and besieged it until September 18th, when Estigarribia surrendered with about 5,500 men. Brazilian control of the river meant that the Paraguayans were surrounded and starved into surrender. The original twelve thousand men had been whittled down by the losses at Yatay and by casualties during the march and siege. All the Allied leaders were there: Mitre of Argentina, Flores of Uruguay, and Dom Pedro II of Brazil—the emperor's only appearance at the front.

López was outraged at the surrender and probably would have had the colonel shot if he had gotten back to Paraguayan lines. Instead, Estigarribia went over to the Allies after the surrender and joined the formation of opponents and turncoats known as the Paraguayan Legion. Some of these Paraguayans fought with the Allies, and their fate was grim if they were captured since they would certainly be executed as traitors. When Asunción finally fell, these and other turncoats formed a provisional Paraguayan government.

The war was not really noticed by the rest of the world at first, except by the British merchants who had interests in the region. The bloody American Civil War was in its final phase. Napoleon III had sent a French force to Mexico and installed a Habsburg grand duke as emperor. Spain had seized the Chincha Islands off Peru in April 1864, and Spain was at war with Peru and Chile. Chancellor Otto von Bismarck of Prussia had begun his calculated wars to establish the German Empire under Prussian leadership with the Austro-Prussian War in 1866. Events in far-off La Plata drew little interest.

The Triple Alliance was almost accidental. Brazil and Argentina were still suspicious of each other, and each continued to have interests in acquiring control over Uruguay. Argentina was brought into the war because Paraguay initiated hostilities. Argentina and Brazil remained uneasy allies for the entire war.

Argentina, Brazil, and Uruguay formally came together in an alliance that came to be called the Triple Alliance, which is the origin of the alternative name for the war (the War of the Triple Alliance). The three allies agreed not to end the war separately and that López had to be removed from power. The Brazilian representatives insisted that Paraguay's national existence should not be threatened. The treaty specified that once Paraguay was defeated, it had to pay the cost of the war through an indemnity.

There was a secret provision in the treaty: both Brazil and Argentina were to gain the territory they had disputed with López, a large slice of Paraguay. Brazil's representative insisted that the treaty specify that Paraguay would not be dismembered as a nation, something that might have happened if Argentina's view had prevailed in the talks. Brazil was by far the most powerful of the three allies and provided the largest number of troops, so the representative got his way. What probably saved Paraguay from extinction after the war was the fact that Argentina and Brazil each saw Paraguay as a buffer against the other.[54]

Paraguay had developed a fairly powerful river navy. In the 1850s, the elder López had tried to develop shipbuilding in Asunción and managed to build at least six river steamers. Their navy consisted of river steamboats, some of them paddlewheels like those on the Mississippi River in the United States. Some of them had

---

[54] Warren, Gaylord. "The Paraguayan Image of the War of the Triple Alliance." *The Americas* 19 (1), July 1962. 3-20. JSTOR access January 12, 2023.

paddlewheels on the sides and some at the stern. Several of the ships were powered by propellers. They were sturdy enough to carry some artillery, but for the most part, the Paraguayan Navy was composed of armed converted merchant steamers. They were not armored.

When the war began in 1864, the Paraguayan Navy consisted of thirty-two assorted river steamers, three steam pinnaces (smaller ships), and about a dozen small *chatas,* which were reinforced by the steamship confiscated from the Brazilians and two ships captured during the occupation of Corrientes. The *chatas* were not powered and had to be towed or rowed. They carried one cannon and floated low in the water. They would only be dangerous up close.

Paraguay had also paid for two double-turreted ironclads, which were under construction in Bordeaux when the war began. These were never delivered, nor were other naval stores and weapons that had been ordered before the war began.[55]

At the start, López had far more men under arms than the Allied armies did in total, but the Brazilians quickly enlarged their army. They already had a large national guard and transferred units of that to their regular army. The war was popular at the beginning, and men readily joined volunteer units. As the war continued on, volunteers became scarcer, so Brazil resorted to forced recruitment of freedmen (freed slaves) and others. However, the strength of its navy made an immediate blockade possible and assured that Allied forces would quickly advance.[56]

It is difficult to look at a campaign and designate a particular battle as being the key to a war's outcome, but virtually all historians agree that the crucial battle of the entire Paraguayan War was a naval battle on the Paraná River, where the small Riachuelo flows into it. The battle took place not far from the city of Corrientes in Argentina and took place in Argentine waters. Corrientes is only a few miles south of where the Paraguay River joins the Paraná, a short trip from the protection of the Humaitá fortress. The nominal commander of the

[55] Ehlers, Hartmut. "The Paraguayan Navy, Past and Present." *Warship International* 41 (1), 2004. 83. JSTOR access, January 12, 2023.

[56] Bethell, Leslie. "The Paraguayan War 1864-70." Pages 99-100 in Leslie Bethell, *Brazil: Essays on History and Politics.* London: University of London Press, 2018.

Paraguayan Navy was one of the dictator's brothers, Benigno López, but the de facto commander was Captain Ignacio Meza. The Paraguayan fleet for this battle consisted of nine steamers of various sizes and several *chatas*, barge-like crafts that were towed. The *chatas* each had one heavy gun, which varied between 80- and 60-pounders.

The ships involved were mostly paddle steamers, but most did not look like the steamboats on North American rivers like the Mississippi and Missouri. These ships had two or three masts, which were typical of ocean-going ships. This battle may have been the largest in history that pitted wooden steamships against each other, although at least one had an iron hull.

The largest Paraguayan warship was the *Tacuarí*, a sidewheel gunboat. She carried two 60-pounders, two 32-pounders, and one 12-pounder breechloader. A 62-pounder cannon would fire a cannonball that weighed approximately sixty-two pounds. Naval artillery could also fire other kinds of shot designed to clear a deck of sailors or to cut and destroy rigging. The breech-loading gun was loaded from the breech, like a rifle, rather than from down the muzzle like other guns. The armament on the *Tacuarí* was formidable and capable of sinking any of the Brazilian ships. All unarmored steamers were highly vulnerable to fire that damaged the paddlewheels. A couple of the Brazilian ships did have some armor, but they were not ironclads. Ironclads showed up later in the war, though.

López ordered his navy to attack the Brazilians. His desired tactic was that the Paraguayans close in on the docked Brazilian ships before dawn and board them. Most of the Brazilian crews would have been asleep on shore or just waking. The Paraguayans were to overwhelm the crews on the steamers, capture the ships, and steam back up to the Humaitá fortress, which was built on a loop in the Paraguay River.

It was supposed to be a surprise attack early in the morning before dawn, but engine trouble on one of the Paraguayan ships delayed the attack, and the damaged steamer did not participate in the battle. Despite the fact that several hours had passed, Captain Meza attacked anyway, probably because there was still some cover on the river from a thick morning fog. The attack was conducted by eight ships and seven small *chatas*. The Paraguayans had the advantage of some nearby shore batteries and two batteries of Congreve rockets.

However, Captain Meza disobeyed orders. Instead of closing in on the Brazilian ships, Meza had his fleet steam downriver in a file, blasting at the Brazilians as they passed. The largest Brazilian ship was a corvette of about a thousand tons called the *Amazonas*. This ship was armed with one 70-pounder and five 68-pounders, which was some formidable artillery. The nine Brazilian steamers ranged considerably in size, like the Paraguayans, but had more and better guns, and the crews were veteran sailors. Meza turned his column around after anchoring the *chatas* at a narrower place in the river and steamed back upstream.

The fighting was intense. The turning point was when the Brazilian commander, Admiral Francisco Barroso, ordered his flagship, the *Amazonas*, to ram the *Paraguari*, a considerably smaller warship. Barroso used his large steamer to ram two more of the Paraguayan ships, crippling them and turning the battle in Brazil's favor. At this point in the battle, the Paraguayans decided to break off, and the remains of their fleet steamed up the Paraguay River to the shelter of Humaitá.[57]

A painting of the Brazilian ships ramming into the Paraguayan fleet during the Battle of Riachuelo.

https://commons.wikimedia.org/wiki/File:Batalha_Naval_do_Riachuelo_Pintura.jpg

---

[57] Military History. "Naval Battle of Riachuelo.".

Paraguay lost four ships, and estimates of Paraguayan casualties range up to 1,500. Brazil lost one ship, the *Jequitinhonha*, and several hundred of its crew, with some losses on other ships in the fleet. The victory gave the Allies complete control of the La Plata and Paraguay river systems almost to the Paraguayan border for the rest of the war. Although the number of lives lost was quite small compared to some of the gory land battles, Riachuelo gave the Allies control of all of the rivers up to the range of artillery from the Humaitá complex, locking Paraguay off from any possible imports of weapons or supplies. The crippled Paraguayan Navy never attacked the Brazilians other than in a few opportunistic raids.

Meza was wounded during the battle and died of his wounds afterward. His disobedience meant that López's strategy of boarding the Brazilian ships was not carried out. The real problem was the attack's delay, which had been caused by a mechanical problem on a ship, which did not participate in the battle. A surprise boarding attack in the very early morning might have succeeded. López was exceedingly angry at the results and remarked that it was a good thing Meza died of a bullet because he would have died from four (the reference being a firing squad). Disobeying orders was sometimes fatal for Paraguayan commanders. López did not permit any officer to attend Meza's funeral.[58]

The Brazilian warships, with minor help from a few Argentine ships, cut Paraguay off from the outside world, but the defenses at Humaitá and the difficulty of river navigation prevented the Brazilian ships from running upriver and landing troops to attack the Paraguayans from the rear.

The Paraguayans evacuated the bit of Argentine territory they occupied when they took the town of Corrientes. Thereafter, Corrientes served as a base for the Allied navy and as a supply and hospital center for the armies. It became kind of a military boom town, and purveyors in sizable numbers came to the city, selling everything from alcohol to sex.

The Allies had complete control of the river downstream from the Paraguayan forts at Humaitá. However, the Brazilian ships were

---

[58] Ibid.

primarily designed for the open ocean, not for fighting in rivers. Several of the Brazilian warships drew too much water to navigate very far upstream in the relatively shallow rivers. The rivers unpredictably changed the main channels, and sandbars appeared and disappeared, something only a river pilot could have been aware of. As the war continued, Brazil added several ironclads to its fleet, including several designed for river fighting. Many of the battles that followed took place near the river, and cannon fire from the ships played a factor in them.

Chapter 10 – The Allies Invade Paraguay

By the beginning of 1866, Paraguay had already suffered somewhere between forty thousand and sixty thousand killed, wounded, missing, and captured, including a large portion of the troops that had been trained and equipped before the war began. Those men could not be easily replaced. The Paraguayans had lost control of the Paraná to the Allied navies (mostly Brazil's navy), and measles and smallpox had appeared. Things did not look particularly good for López and Paraguay.

The Paraguayans retreated from Argentina but maintained their military bearing. During the evacuation of Corrientes, they brought 100,000 cattle back to Paraguay, which helped provision the army. Retreating was not something López often allowed, but he authorized this one. The Allies did not interfere with the evacuation of Corrientes.

Allied troops kept arriving at the front, and Brazil was by far the main supplier of troops. During the war, Brazil mobilized somewhere between 120,000 and 140,000 men, and the Brazilian Navy was the only meaningful naval contingent, blockading the rivers and carrying troops. At the start of the war, Brazil only had about eighteen thousand troops, many of which were stationed in recently restive Rio

Grande do Sul. The country's standing army was increased to about seventy thousand during the first year of the war.[59]

As the war continued, it became less popular. Recruitment centers initially saw a rush of volunteers, but it gradually became difficult for the Allies due to opposition to the war. Paraguay did not have that problem because the long-established system of conscription for public service projects and training helped López sustain his troop numbers. It was also much easier for López to conscript men than in Brazil's much more democratic society.

The Allies had difficulties obtaining recruits later in the war. Recruits from Argentina were sometimes chained together until they arrived at camp. Recruiters in Buenos Aires and Montevideo were known to drug foreigners and deliver them to recruitment stations. Brazil drafted convicts. As in the US Civil War, drafted men could buy substitutes, that is, pay another man to take his place as a draftee. The price for substitutes was high. Brazil offered land to volunteers, and some slaves were freed if they served, although the number actually freed is disputed.[60]

Uruguay was the least effective of the Allies. Not only was Uruguay by far the smallest in population, but it also had difficulty recruiting troops. Flores resorted to recruiting Paraguayan prisoners, who proved to be unreliable. When these men came near Paraguayan lines, many of them deserted. At first, this was extremely dangerous because López often had these Paraguayan deserters shot, but so many deserted their Uruguayan service that López changed his policy.[61]

Allied commanders could be capricious. In February 1865, the Brazilian admiral, Joaquim Marques Lisboa, Marquis of Tamandaré, was on his way to command the Brazilian Navy, but he had a fit over

[59] Bethell, Leslie. "The Paraguayan War 1864-70." Pages 97-98 in Leslie Bethell, *Brazil: Essays on History and Politics.* London: University of London Press, 2018.

[60] Penalta, Alfredo Fornos. "Draft Dodgers, War Resisters, and Turbulent Gauchos: The War of the Triple Alliance Against Paraguay." *Americas* 38 (4) April 1982. 471-72, 475. JSTOR access January 28, 2023.

[61] Whigham, Thomas. *The Road to Armageddon: Paraguay Versus the Triple Alliance, 1864-1870.* Calgary, Alberta: University of Calgary Press, 2017, 18-19.

the price of coal and refused to buy it. His ship had to resort to using its sails and took three weeks to tack up the river to where his command was located. This kind of capriciousness added to the usual problems of three different armies trying to cooperate.

By April, the Allies had amassed an army of forty thousand infantry and fifteen thousand cavalry to invade Paraguay. There were Argentine and Uruguayan units, but the force was largely Brazilian. The troops were both veterans and recent recruits. They were better equipped and clothed than the Paraguayans and probably were better fed. Unlike the Paraguayan Army, these troops had a problem with rivalry among commanders. Some of the Brazilian officers had no experience and minimal competence.

López ordered several attacks as the Allies moved through Corrientes and crossed the Paraná into Paraguay. The region being invaded was north of the Paraná and east of the Paraguay. On April 10th, 1866, the Paraguayans attacked in the Battle of Purutué Bank on the Argentine side of the river and lost the small battle. On April 17th, the Paraguayans' aggressive attacks continued at the Battle of Itapirú, where the four thousand Paraguayan attackers lost five hundred men and the battle to the Brazilians. A typical pattern was for the Paraguayans to launch a fierce attack but suffer heavy casualties from the Allied artillery.

During one of the small yet bloody battles, López disappeared, and the Paraguayans panicked. He had left behind not only his soldiers but also Eliza Lynch and their children. He had gone to an observation post to watch the events. He may or may not have fled out of cowardice, but according to the memoirs of at least one participant, this was an example of López and his usual cowardice.[62]

López was notorious for avoiding danger. He was aware that if he was killed or captured, the Paraguayan War would end then and there, so assessing whether this was cowardice or an excess of caution is impossible to determine. López rarely led his troops in person and had no interest in leading his troops from the front.[63]

---

[62] Ibid, pgs. 39-40.

[63] Ibid.

The Paraguayans kept launching raids and spoiling attacks. On May 2nd, they attacked yet again, pitting a force of some five thousand men against an Argentine and Brazilian force numbering around eight thousand; the result was again a defeat. Called the Battle of Estero Bellaco, the Paraguayans lost 2,500 men, and the Allies lost about 2,000. In this battle, the Paraguayans launched a surprise attack, and they came close to a victory but broke the battle off. They might have inflicted a serious defeat if they had followed through. Both sides suffered horrendous casualties.

The Paraguayans seemed to have particularly hated the Brazilians they were attacking. One cavalry corporal had his horse shot out from under him, but he attacked and killed the enemy, using his flag as a spear. A recurring problem for the Paraguayans was that they had to follow whatever plan López ordered; otherwise, they would face severe consequences, including the possibility of execution. This meant that a commander had little leeway to take advantage of an opportunity that opened up in a battle.[64]

The casualties on both sides in all of these battles were quite high, which was perhaps due to the aggressiveness López expected from his troops. How much of their aggressiveness came from a sense of defending the homeland is not possible to determine because López sometimes reacted to hesitation in battle with executions.

Despite the continuous loss of men, the Paraguayan Army remained formidable, particularly when it came to defense. In the spring of 1866, the British military engineer working for López built a formidable trench system that would allow the Paraguayan forces to defeat any Allied attack.

Instead, López decided to launch a major attack on the morning of May 24th. The night before, he tried to whip up enthusiasm among his troops with speeches. He was apparently good at harangues. In at least one of them, López claimed it was liberty or death and that if the Brazilians won, Paraguay would be destroyed, and the soldiers' wives and children would be sold on the auction block in Rio. López had contempt for the Brazilians, as many Paraguayans and Argentines did at the time. Brazilian slavery was contrasted with the freedom of

---

[64] Ibid, pg. 48-49.

Paraguay, apparently with no sense of irony that López was vastly more of an autocrat than the Brazilian emperor. Whether or not his speeches worked, the Paraguayan Army was spoiling for a fight.

On the morning of May 24th, López launched the biggest Paraguayan attack of the war, with twenty-five thousand Paraguayans smashing into thirty-five thousand Allied troops at the Battle of Tuyutí. The Allied army was again largely Brazilian. It was a closer thing than the final casualty count would indicate. The Paraguayans did very well in the early fighting, but the Brazilian artillery was extremely effective and broke up the attacks. Paraguay had six thousand killed and seven thousand wounded out of a force of twenty-five thousand, and the Allies had about four thousand casualties out of thirty-five thousand engaged. Half the Paraguayan Army became casualties, an extraordinarily high casualty rate for any army in any war. The proportion of dead to wounded in the Paraguayan ranks was also extraordinary.

This defeat cost López a large percentage of his remaining veteran soldiers. It was also difficult to replace weapons and other equipment. In the months following the disaster, López called up all the reserves, and a large number of all able-bodied men left the country to replace the losses. About twenty thousand men eventually gathered at Humaitá, traveling by steamer on the rivers that Paraguay still controlled.

Figures for Paraguay's strength are, at best, approximate. Given a population of supposedly no more than 400,000, which would have totaled about 100,000 adult men, López's ability to keep calling up recruits after huge losses, even if many were old men and boys, was phenomenal. It also suggests that the estimate of 400,000 Paraguayans is too low.

López replaced the casualties with raw recruits, but there was no way to replace the lost weapons and other equipment, as well as the experience of the veteran units and their officers who had been killed. Tuyutí was probably the largest battle ever fought between nations in all of South America's history. The eighteen or nineteen thousand total casualties echoed the losses of some of the larger battles in the Civil War in the United States. This battle ended the possibility that López could launch another big offensive campaign.

Despite this disaster, the defeat was not an utter catastrophe for Paraguay. The Paraguayans were resilient and proved formidable in defense. Humaitá proved to be an insurmountable obstacle for many months. Among other defenses at Humaitá were three massive chains stretched across navigable channels to prevent Allied warships from going upriver.

The Paraguay River was a challenge for ships, even without the formidable Paraguayan defensive artillery. The river was characterized by irregular flows, which means the depth fluctuated, sometimes resulting in insufficient water to float larger ships. The river had braided channels with innumerable side channels, oxbow lakes, and bayous. The shorelines were often characterized by swamps that were dense with grasses and canes, making it difficult terrain for infantrymen and even more difficult for horsemen. The main channel at Humaitá was only a few hundred yards wide, and the chains and cannons were tough obstacles.

The Paraguayan fortress was not the only factor impeding the Allied use of their naval strength. Argentine President and General Mitre was in overall command at times, and the Brazilian naval commander, Joaquim Marques Lisboa, Marquis of Tamandaré, did not approve. Tamandaré, as he is known, was strongly opposed to letting an Argentine landlubber command his fleet. These issues of who should command what force continued and handicapped Allied cooperation.[65]

The situation of the common soldiers was typically not very good. Supplies for the Allied soldiers had to be shipped upriver from Brazil, which made for quite a long supply line. Some supplies could come from Uruguay and Rio Grande do Sul, but the roads were so bad that any supplies had to be shipped by water. The Allies tended to feed their troops rations of biscuits, *charqui*, and yerba mate. The *charqui* and mate were common on both sides, but the Paraguayans ate manioc as their main food. A Guaraní soldier was reputed to be able to survive for days on just a little manioc.

The main battlefields in 1866 and 1867 were in the region between Corrientes and the Paraguayan fortress of Humaitá, some miles

---

[65] Ibid, 19-20.

upstream from where the Paraguay flows into the Paraná. The battlegrounds were typically marshy, sometimes swamps, with jungly brush and dense stands of trees, cane, and thorn thickets. Rain and mud often made life miserable for the soldiers on both sides. Sanitation was often rudimentary, and diseases like malaria sickened thousands of men. The main killer was probably dysentery, which was the big killer in encampments in the US Civil War and killed thousands of troops in the Crimean War. Snakes were plentiful, and the alligator-like caimans could be dangerous.

Conditions for the wounded were abysmal. The Allies built reasonably good medical facilities in Corrientes, and a Brazilian steamer was converted into a hospital ship. There was an acute shortage of doctors, and they had little in the way of medicines to work with. They did have more medicine than the Paraguayans, although the Paraguayans apparently did well with traditional medicines made from herbs. The troops began to be equipped with rifles that fired the heavy bullet called the Minié ball, a rifled bullet named after its French inventor that caused gory wounds. The Minié ball had been used extensively by both sides in the US Civil War, causing thousands of amputations. When a Minié ball hits a body, it shatters bone and creates deep wounds. The Allied doctors performed amputations with scalpels and bone saws; the Paraguayans did amputations more often by machete. A high proportion of the wounded died.[66]

---

[66] Ibid, 52-53.

Chapter 11 – Bloodbaths, a Stalemate, and Paraguay's Gibraltar

The Allies had been confident of a victory after they invaded Paraguay. After the Allied victory at Tuyutí, they became even more confident of ending the war soon. The immediate problem was the unfriendly Paraguayan terrain and the strong fortress complex at Humaitá. At the time, the complex was compared to Gibraltar, the massive British fortress at the entrance to the Mediterranean, and to Sebastopol, the Russian fortress that stoutly resisted the Allies in the Crimean War. Humaitá lived up to the comparisons, blocking the Allies from advancing deeper into Paraguay for the better part of two years. Most of the big battles of the war were fought near or at the fortress complex. Perhaps 100,000 lives were lost there.

The Paraguayan Army proved to be remarkably resilient, even after the disaster at Tuyutí. They beat back Allied attacks at the Battle of Boquerón on July 16th, 1866, and at the Battle of Sauce on July 18th. These defeats cost the Allies about six thousand casualties compared to two thousand for Paraguay. The Paraguayans were almost always aggressive and tended to suffer heavy casualties during attacks but were in prepared positions when on the defensive, making them extremely difficult to overcome.

Humaitá was built on the east bank of the Paraguay River a few miles above its confluence with the Paraná. The Paraguay River makes a sharp curve there, and the river's main channel narrows to about two hundred yards. Some of the artillery battery positions were built on a bluff about thirty feet high, giving the men at the fort a considerable advantage over any ships in the river.

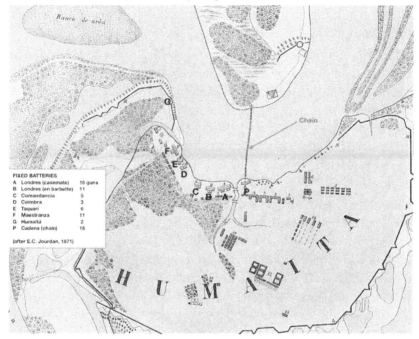

A survey of the batteries at Humaitá.
https://commons.wikimedia.org/wiki/File:Batteries_of_Humait%C3%A1_fortress.png

Construction began in 1854 but was made a priority after the 1855 incident when the Brazilian flotilla threatened Asunción and after 1859, when the Americans came to demand an apology and reparations for the sailor killed by the Paraguayans firing on the US warship *Water Witch* in 1855.

Humaitá had half a dozen artillery batteries, several of them in fixed positions in casemates (protective emplacements). One of the batteries had sheltering walls that were twenty-eight feet thick. The initial design was apparently by a Hungarian military engineer who had entered Paraguayan service, Francisco Wisner de Morganstern. The number of artillery pieces is not known, but it was certainly more than one hundred. Humaitá was protected from attacks from behind by several natural features, including swamps and lagoons that were almost impassible.

The Allies scored a victory on September 3rd when they attacked the Paraguayan batteries at Curuzú, part of the very large defense complex in front of Humaitá. Curuzú was in a formidable position, protecting a large area near the fortress called the quadrilateral from landings from the river. The quadrilateral consisted of trenches, barriers, and field artillery batteries.

The Allied strategy was to land troops from ships while attacking Curuzú from the nearby Allied lines. Brazilian warships shelled the Paraguayan position from the river, and 8,000 Allied troops charged the defensive position, capturing it and inflicting 2,500 casualties to 800 of their own. Several Paraguayan units broke and ran, which was very unusual for Paraguayan units on the defensive. This battle was the occasion when Paraguayan mines sank the Brazilian ironclad *Rio de Janeiro.*

After the battle, López was furious and accused his troops of cowardice. He imposed the ancient Roman punishment of decimation on the 10th Battalion, in which one soldier in ten was executed. Soldiers and officers drew straws, and the losers were executed. In the Roman practice, the nine members of a ten-man squad who did not draw the losing straw killed the loser. If they refused to kill the loser, they were killed. López apparently used firing squads. More than sixty soldiers and officers from the unit were executed for cowardice on this occasion.[67]

The area in front of the fortress complex was protected by an elaborate series of trenches and field fortifications. It was called the quadrilateral and totaled a dozen miles of fortified line. This defensive line was designed by George Thompson, a British military engineer hired by the Paraguayans and trusted by López. Thompson was an officer in the army and highly skilled at creating defensive works. The size of the Paraguayan garrison in the quadrilateral and the fort complex is not known for sure, but it may have been as many as eighteen thousand. The quality of the artillery varied a great deal.

[67] Whigham, Thomas. *The Road to Armageddon: Paraguay Versus the Triple Alliance, 1864-1870.* Calgary, Alberta: University of Calgary Press, 2017, 100-101.

Some were relatively modern, purchased from abroad just before the war, some had been forged in the armory at Asunción, and some were inherited from Spanish times. After the fort fell, a British observer wrote that he found two old Spanish cannons that carried the dates 1671 and 1684.[68]

On September 12th, 1866, a most unusual event occurred. López and the president of Argentina, Bartolomé Mitre, who was also the commanding general of the Argentine and Allied forces, and Flores, the Uruguayan president and army commander, held a meeting at a place called Yatayí Corá. López had invited them to a parley.

López knew that the war was going against Paraguay, and he offered major concessions to end the war, including territories. López's requirements for the possible concessions required that he continue to lead Paraguay and that Paraguay would not be divided among the three allies. Mitre and Flores rejected the conditions López proposed. The treaty initiating the Triple Alliance specified that the war would not end until López was driven from power.[69]

The president and the dictator met outdoors. Mitre brought a guard of twenty cavalry lancers, and López apparently discreetly posted a squad of sharpshooters nearby. Neither leader seems to have contemplated using the occasion to murder the other. A charge by the lancers would probably have ended the war and saved tens of thousands of lives. But in that era, a parley was honored, even with a leader as detested as López.

López had his staff bring chairs, and the two men sat and talked. Mitre summoned Flores, the Uruguayan president and commander, who was little interested in the possibilities. The conversation lasted for five hours. Apparently, the conversation was friendly, and the men chatted about war and books. There was no progress on substantive issues. The escorts for the two commanders mixed and also talked. Everyone was surprisingly friendly, considering the bitterness of the fighting. López gave Mitre a choice Paraguayan cigar, and they parted

---

[68] Wikiwand. "Fortress of Humaitá."
https://www.wikiwand.com/en/Fortress_of_Humait%C3%A1 Retrieved January 24, 2023.

[69] Bethell, Leslie. "The Paraguayan War 1864-70." Page 101 in Leslie Bethell, *Brazil: Essays on History and Politics*. London: University of London Press, 2018.

amicably. However, Mitre declared himself bound by the 1865 treaty that formed the Triple Alliance. The Brazilians had no interest in the meeting, having decided that eliminating López as leader of Paraguay was their most important goal.[70]

Mitre (1821–1906) was an unusual man. He was born in Buenos Aires to a Greek immigrant family. He lived in Uruguay for a time, served in the Uruguayan army, and was active in Uruguayan politics. He was active in politics for three generations and served as president of Argentina and commanding general of Argentine troops in the Paraguayan War. He was also a journalist, writer, and poet. His long life and literary skills shaped how Argentine historians later viewed López and the war.

After the Allied victory at Curuzú, where they had taken the Paraguayan batteries, the Allies became overconfident and planned a more general attack that they were sure would result in the conquest of Humaitá and probably end the war. On September 22nd, they attacked the Paraguayan fortifications at Curupayty, another bastion of the massive Humaitá complex. The Allies fully expected to take it as they had taken the Curuzú fortifications a few days previously.

The cannon emplacements were not the only defense. López was willing to consider unusual ideas, including what were called torpedoes at that time (today, we would call them contact mines). In July 1866, several officers gathered to figure out how to make "torpedoes." The idea seems to have originated with an American employed by López, a man named William Kruger. He had apparently had some experience using these devices in the American Civil War. Kruger, George Masterman, and others devised an effective contact fuse so the mines would blow up when they made contact with an enemy ship. Masterman was British. He was employed as the chief pharmacist for the army, so he was in charge of medicines. His expertise in chemistry was thought to be helpful. The mines were passive; they were designed to float downstream and explode on contact with whatever they hit. The Paraguayans seemed to have had enough gunpowder to make many of these mines. Kruger

---

[70] Whigham, Thomas. *The Road to Armageddon: Paraguay Versus the Triple Alliance, 1864-1870*. Calgary, Alberta: University of Calgary Press, 2017, 105-106.

and a Paraguayan associate died in an accidental explosion.[71]

The mines were released upstream to float down the current in the hope they would hit a Brazilian ship. They were not just exercises; one mine sank the 1,000-ton Brazilian ironclad warship *Rio de Janeiro*, killing its captain and most of the crew in the process. The devices could also be anchored to the river bottom as a deterrent to warships wanting to steam upriver. The mines sank only one Brazilian warship, but that was enough to make the Brazilian captains wary and kept them down the river far enough to affect their ability to shell Paraguayan targets.[72]

The attack on Curupayty was preceded by hours of shelling from the Brazilian ironclad warships on the river, but they had to be careful of Humaitá's artillery, and the captains continued to be wary of mines. As it was, the ironclad *Brasil* was hit dozens of times by shells from the fort. The other ironclads were also hit but did not suffer as much damage. Some sailors aboard the bombarding ships were killed by the counterfire. The Brazilian ships fired more than five thousand rounds in an attempt to disrupt the Paraguayans and destroy the artillery emplacements. The Paraguayans picked up some of the enemy cannonballs that landed harmlessly and later used them in their own cannons. The five-hour naval bombardment was totally ineffective.

About twenty thousand troops, Argentine and Brazilian, formed up and attacked the bastion, intending to storm it. The Paraguayans had prepared for the assault. Under Thompson's instructions, they had dug trenches to protect their own infantry and to stall an enemy advance. They created barbed-wire-like defenses of limbs and branches full of thorns (barbed wire had not yet been invented) and lanes for clear artillery and rifle fire. The terrain in front of the batteries was already difficult because much of it was swampy, wet, and muddy.

---

[71] Ibid, pgs. 92-93.

[72] Wikiwand. "Fortress of Humaitá."
https://www.wikiwand.com/en/Fortress_of_Humait%C3%A1 . Retrieved January 24, 2023.

A painting of the Battle of Curupayty.
https://commons.wikimedia.org/wiki/File:C%C3%A1ndido_Lopez_-
Trinchera_de_Curupayt%C3%AD_-_Google_Art_Project_(497159).jpg

As the Allied troops advanced, they were mowed down by the Paraguayan artillery, such as big caliber guns using grapeshot at almost point-blank range. Paraguayan musket volleys swept the battlefield, and the Paraguayans also fired Congreve rockets at the attackers. Some attacking regiments were decimated yet were ordered to attack again. Friendly fire from the fleet killed some of the attackers, and in other incidents, attackers were shot down from the flank by other Allied troops that mistook them for Paraguayan units. Finally, the attack was called off. The Curupayty battery remained in Paraguayan hands.

The Allies had grossly underestimated the Paraguayans. Paraguay's best general, José Díaz, was in command. Díaz had no military experience before the war began, but he emerged as an aggressive and canny commander. Instead of the anticipated victory, the attackers were shot to pieces as they made attack after attack. The battle was made worse by Díaz's poor leadership.

The attacks failed, and the Allies returned to where they had started from. They suffered somewhere between 6,000 and 8,000 casualties to Paraguay's 190. Curupayty was the most severe defeat of the war for the Triple Alliance and the greatest victory for López and his army.

The Allied troops' morale had been sky-high after the win at Curuzú but nearly collapsed after this defeat. Defeatism spread among the troops, and when news of the defeat reached Brazil and Argentina, criticism of the war and leadership reached new peaks. The Allied leadership was badly shaken, and the defeat stalled their offensive for many months, although things would change in July 1867.

At Curupayty, the dead and wounded littered the battlefield. Many wounded drowned when they fell in waist-deep swamps and marshes. The Paraguayans stripped the dead of anything useful, from shoes and boots to sidearms, ammunition, and clothing. They tossed the dead into river lagoons and, in a macabre action, tied corpses together in chains and tossed them into the river to drift down.[73]

After the disaster, the veteran Brazilian general, Luís Alves de Lima e Silva, Duke of Caxias, was sent to the front by Dom Pedro, where he became an effective commander. When Caxias arrived, he set about restructuring the Allied army. Over the months, he cashiered some of the inept Brazilian commanders, promoted others, and worked on lessening the toll taken by disease by improving sanitation and improving medical care. Unlike many commanders, he was genuinely concerned about the morale of the troops. Morale slowly recovered. Caxias also began developing a strategy that he thought would defeat Humaitá, which would allow them to go on to capture Asunción and end the war.

Humaitá's formidable artillery was not the only problem for the Allies. The obvious strategy was one that was impossible at first: the Brazilian Navy running ships past the fortress and landing troops upstream to cut the complex off from resupply from Asunción. Aside from the danger posed by contact mines, the defenses included a thick chain boom that blocked the river. This chain was made from several smaller chains and floated on pontoons and small boats, with winches on shore that lowered or raised it.

There were other oddities during the long standoff at Humaitá. López had newspapers printed for the troops in both Spanish and Guaraní. A supply of newsprint was not available, so the resourceful Paraguayans used fibers from a kind of wild pineapple to make paper. The British engineer Thompson managed to set up several short telegraph lines so that observers in different parts of the quadrilateral could send reports in Morse code to López, who reportedly frequently read them in his fortified command center.[74]

[73] Whigham, Thomas. *The Road to Armageddon: Paraguay Versus the Triple Alliance, 1864-1870.* Calgary, Alberta: University of Calgary Press, 2017, 118.

[74] Wikiwand. "Fortress of Humaitá." wikiwand.com.en/Fortress_of_Humaitá/. Retrieved

Another oddity was the Brazilian interest in observation balloons. Dom Pedro was very interested in current events and science and had read about the use of observation balloons in the US Civil War. His administrators brought in a French balloonist in October 1866, but as the balloon was being unpacked from its crates, it caught fire. Balloons were highly flammable because of the materials they were constructed from and the highly flammable hydrogen used to carry them aloft.

In March 1867, Brazil's ambassador to the United States invited the former head of the Union Army's balloon program, Thaddeus Lane, to come to Brazil with balloons that could be used at the front. Lane declined but recommended two balloonists who had worked for him: the brothers James and Edward Lane. The brothers accepted Brazil's invitation and arrived at the Brazilian Army's encampment in late May 1867. They brought two balloons with them, one that could carry two observers and one that could carry six. There was an immediate problem. Hydrogen was generated from sulfuric acid and iron filings, and supplies of these were supposed to have been shipped from the US but weren't. The brothers had to scour La Plata but managed to find what they needed.

The first ascent carried a Paraguayan turncoat who was familiar with the Paraguayan defensive lines and a Polish soldier of fortune, a military engineer, who drew several highly useful maps of the Paraguayan fortifications. Future ascents were less useful, partly because the Paraguayans made fires that generated a great deal of smoke to hide their positions from the balloonists. After twenty ascents, the American brothers went home to New England in September. They were well paid for their efforts.[75]

Sanitation and personal hygiene on both sides were rudimentary. Medical knowledge of the causes of disease was beginning to make some progress, and the lessons of the Crimean War and the American Civil War showed that efforts to improve the conditions of

---

January 24, 2023.

[75] Whigham, Thomas. "Brazil's Balloon Corps. Pride, Desperation and the Limits of Military Intelligence in the Triple Alliance War." *Luso-Brazilian Review* 52 (2), 2015. 9-10. JSTOR access January 12, 2023.

---

soldiers and the wounded could save lives. Still, the war was brutal, and sometimes, the piles of dead were simply tossed into a river. Prisoners of war who had cholera were sometimes abandoned when detachments moved camps. Brazil had its own version of the Crimean War's Florence Nightingale, Anna Néri (1814–1880). Néri had two sons in the war and went to the front as a nurse. She was so effective that Dom Pedro later gave her a pension for life.[76]

Meanwhile, turmoil continued in Uruguay. Ex-president Bernardo Berro rebelled against Flores, the Colorado politician the Brazilians had backed. Berro had requested that López help him resist Flores and the Brazilians, but López couldn't reach Uruguay, and Berro lost. Flores was assassinated in February 1868, and on the same day, Berro was captured and killed. The civil strife reduced Uruguay, the junior partner in the Triple Alliance, to an insignificant participant. It is not known if López had helped Berro to rebel. Flores's death did not affect the Allies because he had not been a particularly effective commander when he led troops.

Encouraged by the victory at Curupayty, López continued his aggressive tactics. On November 3rd, 1867, the Paraguayans, with nine thousand men under General Vicente Barrios, attacked the Allies. The attack was to coordinate cavalry circling around the Allies to attack them from the flank, but that did not work. The Paraguayans broke the Allied lines and reached the camp and supply dumps, which were looted and seriously damaged. However, the Brazilian artillery was extremely effective and cut down the attackers in droves. The Paraguayans abandoned the battlefield. The Second Battle of Tuyutí was again a defeat for the Paraguayans, who left behind three thousand dead.

Winning the war required getting warships past Humaitá and opening the way to Asunción. Getting the Brazilian ironclads past the fortress's guns required three things: a high enough water level in the river to float the warships, getting rid of the chain boom, and finding an opportune moment to run the warships past the range of the guns

---

[76] Fioravanti, Carlos. "The Scourge of Disease During the Paraguayan War." *Pesquisa* Issue 309, 2021. https://revistapesquisa.fapesp.br/en/the-scourge-of-disease-during-the-paraguayan-war/ . Retrieved January 13, 2023.

at Humaitá.

The Brazilians paid attention to the events of the US Civil War and noted its inconclusive battle in March 1862 when the Confederate ironclad *Merrimac* (the ship's formal name was the CSS *Virginia*) fought the novel Union ironclad *Monitor*. The *Monitor* introduced the rotating turret to the naval world, and the Brazilian Navy liked the idea. They built several *Monitor*-like ships with shallow drafts specifically for battles on the rivers. The warships were built at the shipyards in Rio and joined the fleet near Humaitá in February 1868.

It took several months, but Brazilian naval gunners kept firing on the pontoons and other supports for the chain boom. Finally, they sank all of the pontoons and support boats, and the chain sank to the river bottom, rendered useless as a block in the river. On the night of February 19th, 1868, the depth of the Paraguay River peaked, and six Brazilian ironclads steamed upriver and passed the range of the Humaitá guns. The passage was a grave risk, and the Brazilians thought they might lose one or more ships. As it happened, their armor was sufficient enough to make the Paraguayan fire irrelevant. The ships got plenty of dents in the armor but suffered only ten wounded. There had been a diversionary attack on land, with the Allies losing a thousand men.

This exploit resembled the Union fleet on the Mississippi passing the Confederate fortress at Vicksburg in the summer of 1863 during the US Civil War. It is not known whether the Vicksburg action inspired the Brazilian action. Humaitá seems to have been more formidable than Vicksburg. The Brazilian ironclads north of Humaitá were the beginning of the end for the fortress.

This action by the Brazilian Navy almost immediately became legendary and came to be called the "Passage of Humaitá." The passage was done in three stages of pairs of two ships each, one an armored steamship and the other a turreted river monitor. The Passage of Humaitá was almost as important as the Battle of Riachuelo in 1865 because it eventually led to cutting Humaitá off from Asunción and López abandoning the city. The Passage of Humaitá was greeted with celebrations in Brazil, and support for the war increased.

A painting of the Passage of Humaitá by Victor Meirelles.
https://commons.wikimedia.org/wiki/File:Passagem_de_Humayt%C3%A1.jpg

The fighting on the water continued in a rather odd way. On March 2nd, the Paraguayans tried a surprise night attack on two of the Brazilian ironclads that had passed by Humaitá, the *Lima Barros* and *Cabral*. The Paraguayans moved quietly to achieve a surprise attack with 1,500 men in a flotilla of canoes. They were armed primarily with cutlasses and machetes. They swarmed the two Brazilian warships and engaged in desperate hand-to-hand fighting.

The attack was broken up with the aid of two other warships that fired grapeshot at close range. The Paraguayan attack was beaten back, with the Paraguayans losing several hundred attackers and many of their canoes. The novelty of men in canoes armed with cutlasses attacking ironclad warships is colorful, but it also shows the Paraguayans' desperation. The Paraguayan Navy still had a steamer or two left but was helpless to resist the Brazilian fleet except by nuisance attacks and mines.

Early in 1868, Caxias was ready for his campaign to end the war. He sidestepped Humaitá by advancing farther east and north of the fortress complex, a flanking maneuver coordinated with an Argentine movement on the west side of the river.

Stubborn Paraguayan resistance continued, and once again, the impressive Thompson created a very strong defensive line that probably would have stopped Caxias's advance. However, Caxias declined to attack the position from the front and instead took advantage of the Allies' control of the river to apply a novel strategy. He sent his engineers across the river to build a log road through a swamp. When it was completed, he moved most of his army across the river to the west side, marched up the log road, recrossed the river, and attacked the almost impregnable Paraguayan position from the rear. This sparked a series of small but savage battles. The Paraguayan troops suffered thousands of casualties and withdrew in the direction of Asunción. Humaitá still loomed over the river, but Allied troops were to the north and nearly had it surrounded. López managed to successfully pull most of the Humaitá troops out of Caxias's trap but left a small garrison there, which surrendered on July 25th, 1868. López had ordered the remaining troops to fight to the death, so he was outraged when the starving troops gave up.

Caxias stopped his advance for a time to prepare for a final advance on Asunción. Brazilian warships had already reached the capital city and shelled it, but it would take the army to quell all Paraguayan resistance and completely occupy it.

By December of 1868, the Allies had more than fifty thousand troops and a very strong naval presence at the front. López had few resources left and resorted to conscripting slaves and teenagers. So many men had been drafted and fallen that women were virtually the only labor force in agriculture and what was left of trade. They also had an important role in the army's support services. There were few men to plow and harvest or drive oxcarts to supply the army, so there was less food.

By the end of the war, a very large percentage of Paraguayan men had been killed, with some estimates as high as 90 percent. Women, boys, and old men who were not conscripted were the agricultural force; they planted, plowed, yoked, and drove oxen. They slaughtered animals, processed meat, and did all the other tasks of a farmhand. Women were mobilized to produce uniforms for the army. Due to the shortage of cotton and wool, they made uniforms from coconut fiber and fibers from a wild pineapple. Women were also encouraged to donate their jewelry and other valuables to the cause.[77]

---

[77] Ganson, Barbara. "Following the Children into Battle: Women at War in Paraguay, 1864-

Women were also with all the Paraguayan Army detachments. They washed uniforms, nursed the wounded, cooked corn meal and cassava, dug trenches, served as teamsters, gathered firewood, buried the dead, prepared mate, and rolled cigars.[78]

1870." *The Americas* 46 (3), January 1990. 349-350. JSTOR access January 12, 2023.

[78] Ibid, pg. 356.

Chapter 12 – Guerrilla War and Tragedy

The fall of Humaitá did not end the war, and Asunción did not immediately fall. The Allies gradually advanced but did so carefully. They continued to suffer losses from disease and Paraguayan resistance. Caxias led the mostly Brazilian troops in the final campaign, the *Campanha da Dezembrada* (the December Campaign), which he assumed would end the war.

In December 1868, the Paraguayans repeatedly attacked the advancing Allied force. The Brazilian Navy controlled the river and could shell positions to help the forces on land. With increasing desperation, the Paraguayans attacked in the battles of Ytororó, Avaí, and Lomas Valentinas. The Battle of Lomas Valentinas lasted from December 21^s to the 27th. In this third battle, about three thousand troops, led by López himself, engaged ten thousand Brazilians. The fighting was savage, with some of it being hand-to-hand. The Brazilians suffered about three thousand casualties, but the Paraguayan force was virtually destroyed. In these last battles, an astonishingly high percentage of the Paraguayan attackers were killed. During this December campaign, what remained of the Paraguayan Army was annihilated. Caxias sent a letter to López demanding surrender, but López refused. López escaped the battlefield and evaded Brazilian patrols, escaping with his bodyguard and some family to the hills to the east.

Allied troops occupied Asunción on January 1st, 1869. The bulk of the Allied army entered Asunción on January 5th, 1869. Caxias decided his contribution to the war was enough and resigned from his position on January 15th. Emperor Pedro reluctantly accepted the resignation and replaced Caxias with Prince Gaston, Count of Eu, his son-in-law.

Gaston (1842–1922) was French-born and a member of the French aristocracy. Despite his age, he was a veteran soldier. He had served in North Africa in a war in Morocco and with Brazilian units. He was quite young for a theater command, and his kinship with Dom Pedro probably was why he was appointed. However, Gaston turned out to be an extremely able commander, although he was accused of ruthlessness. His assignment was to run López to ground and either capture or kill him. Gaston did so, but the task took more than a year.

López fled to the mountains and started to recruit yet another army, although it was mostly boys and old men who were poorly armed and poorly trained. By this time, the Paraguayans had little left other than López's ruthlessness and grim determination and the sense of fighting off Paraguay's destruction, which seems to have helped to motivate the desperate attacks. Despite the Allied occupation of Paraguay's capital and heartland, and despite the vast number of deaths, the dictator was somewhat successful in recruiting another force.

As the war winded down, López became increasingly paranoid about plots. In 1868, López discovered another plot against him. It may have been real, or like other plots, it may have been the result of one or more suspects implicating others while under torture. His paranoia seems to have gotten progressively worse, and the net of presumed conspiracies spread wide. Hundreds of people were tortured, and many of them were killed. Those López had executed for presumed treason or for defeatism include his brothers, Benigno and Venancio, and both his brothers-in-law, General Berro and Saturnino Bedoya.[79]

[79] Kennedy, Thomas. *Jose Gaspar Rodriguez de Francia and Francisco Solano López, as Historical Heroes.* Thesis, Texas Tech University, 1974, 64.

It's frequently alleged that López had his mother and both his sisters tortured under suspicion they were involved in plots against him. Whether he did or not is uncertain, so the story may be another attempt to tarnish his name, or it may be another fact in his considerable infamy. There is no doubt that hundreds of Paraguayans were executed or tortured to death as a result of his paranoia in this sad episode and later, and there is no doubt that the performance of Paraguayan forces was affected by the executions of experienced commanders. It resembles the kind of purge conducted on a much larger scale by a later dictator, Joseph Stalin, who purged most of the Soviet senior army commanders before the German invasion.

The remains of the once-powerful Paraguayan Navy retreated far up the Paraguay River and into a creek flowing into it. There were six steamers left. They were left helpless when water levels lowered, and their cannons were sent south to help with land combat. The remaining crews had nothing to defend their ships but a few muskets. When Brazilian troops came close, the crews blew up the boilers, scuttled the steamers, and scattered to avoid capture. The remains of the ships remained in the bayou for decades.[80]

This last phase of the war is often called the Campaign of the Hills or the Cordillera Campaign because the theater of the war shifted from Humaitá and the rivers to the hills and mountains east and northeast of Asunción. The hunt for López was almost entirely a Brazilian affair. Some twenty thousand to twenty-five thousand Allied troops remained in Paraguay after the capture of Asunción. Many were used to garrison Asunción and ensure the new government's compliance, but thousands of troops were sent to hunt down the dictator. How many troops López had is not known for certain, but he managed to find substantial numbers. They could not have been well armed, and most of the veteran officers had died of combat or disease, been executed, or been captured.

López managed to again create a small Paraguayan force, mostly consisting of conscripted and volunteer teenagers and boys. By this point in the war, a very large percentage of grown men in Paraguay

---

[80] Whigham, Thomas. *The Road to Armageddon: Paraguay Versus the Triple Alliance, 1864-1870*. Calgary, Alberta: University of Calgary Press, 2017, 386.

had died, so there were few veteran soldiers left in the new army. This nine-thousand-man force seems to have few grown men in it. Some of the Paraguayan soldiers were as young as ten, and almost all of them were hungry and barefoot. The situation is comparable to the last days of the Third Reich when the fabled German Army was reduced to drafting teens and boys. The Paraguayans resisted fiercely and were slaughtered by the veteran Brazilian troops.

On August 12th, 1869, portions of this new army were protecting the small town of Piribebuy, which was López's makeshift capital. Brazilian scouts located López there. The Brazilians gathered twenty thousand soldiers and attacked. The 1,600 Paraguayan defenders were surprised by the attack and were nearly annihilated; they resisted fiercely but suffered very heavy casualties. This was called a battle, but it was so one-sided that it was little more than a massacre. López once again escaped the Brazilian patrols.

A few days later, on August 16th, a force of 3,500 Paraguayans was attacked by about 20,000 Brazilian and Argentine troops at the Battle of Campo Grande (also called the Battle of Acosta Nu). As many as two thousand Paraguayans were killed. The Paraguayans killed around two hundred of their attackers. The battle was also closer to a massacre than a battle. The Paraguayan boys and teenagers were poorly armed, and many were barefoot. Some begged for mercy but were cut down anyway. López escaped once more.

A painting of the Battle of Campo Grande by Pedro Américo.
https://commons.wikimedia.org/wiki/File:Batalha_de_Campo_Grande_-_1871.jpg

The last months of the resistance are not well known. A new government was formed in Asunción, largely by exiled opponents of the López regime and some who had been captured in the war and joined the Allies. López ruled little more than the ground his guards walked on, yet he continued to prolong the resistance, and the war continued. Gaston, Count of d'Eu, drove his men relentlessly in the search for López and the end of the war.

López seems to have retreated even deeper into paranoia and became even more cruel and vindictive. He drank heavily and brooded over treason. One probably false accusation of treason came from a soldier accused of wanting to assassinate the dictator. Under torture, the soldier implicated members of the presidential guard and others. López reacted with his usual fury. He had eighty-six enlisted men and sixteen officers executed, a large number, considering how few troops he had left. Those were not the only executions. Yet hundreds of soldiers remained loyal as they stumbled through the brush and the streambeds, barefoot and starving. There had to be something more than sheer terror holding the little force together; maybe it was López's personal magnetism, or maybe it was a sense of Paraguay being doomed.

Again and again, López escaped Brazilian troops with his consort, Eliza Lynch, a few other associates, and some of his bodyguards, totaling in all a few hundred people. Despite the slaughter of his last army, López was not run to ground for several more months. Finally, López and his bodyguard, consisting of about four hundred troops, encamped at a remote place called Cerro Corá. A large Brazilian cavalry detachment found them on March 1ˢᵗ, 1870.

This Battle of Cerro Corá was another engagement that was more a massacre than a battle. About half the four hundred Paraguayan troops were killed, and half were captured. López refused to surrender. He pulled out his revolver but was lanced by a Brazilian corporal, Francisco Lacerda. The dictator managed to reach the shore of a stream but was found. When he refused to surrender, he was shot in the back by a Brazilian soldier named João Soares. The commander had placed a bounty of £120 on López, dead or alive. Who got that large bounty is not known.

The Paraguayan War ended as it began: a drama with López as the principal actor.

A painting of the death of Francisco Solano López.
https://commons.wikimedia.org/wiki/File:Muerte_de_L%C3%B3pez_en_R%C3%ADo_Aqui
dab%C3%A1n..jpg

In a scene with intense melodrama, Eliza Lynch was either with López or nearby when he died. López had been mortally wounded by a horseman's lance and managed to get to the side of a river, apparently to try to swim away. He refused to surrender and was shot dead, saying, "With me, Paraguay dies." His dying words may have been those defiant ones or some version of them. They also might be patriotic fiction. But when cornered by the Brazilian lancers, López actually seems to have sworn at them in racist terms of contempt, calling them monkeys and worse.

López's oldest son, who was fifteen, had been made a colonel in the army by his father. He was ordered to surrender and shouted, "A Paraguayan colonel never surrenders!" and was shot on the spot. Eliza stood over her son's body and said bitterly to the Brazilian officers, "Is this the civilization you promised?" which was a reference to the Allied propaganda that the purpose of the war was to bring civilization to Paraguay by replacing its mad dictator.[81]

---

[81] Wikipedia. "Eliza Lynch (1833-1886)."https://en.wikipedia.org/wiki/Eliza_Lynch "
Retrieved January 13, 2023.

She somehow dug a shallow grave with her hands, one big enough to hold both her oldest son and her partner, López.[82]

That's the melodramatic end. López's actual end may not have been as heroic, although many of the articles and books about his death describe the dictator's end that way. To some historians, López seems to have been deeply flawed but to have died a hero's death. Others see him as a miserable paranoid coward who died the dog's death he richly deserved.

According to one preeminent historian of the Paraguayan War, Eliza Lynch and her children boarded a carriage and left the scene. When they were overtaken by Brazilian lancers, the carriage stopped, and the occupants got out. The fifteen-year-old son was laughed at and made his defiant "A Paraguayan colonel does not surrender!" and reached for his pistol, at which point he was lanced to death. His eleven-year-old brother was there and was killed as well, apparently in cold-blooded murder—this is not mentioned in some of the history books, so it might not have happened. But the rest, including López's mother, were given guards and treated well. Soldiers were assigned to help Eliza dig the graves for her husband and sons, unlike the story of her digging the grave with her bare hands.[83]

Eliza was not mistreated, and she may have had some jewels or other valuables with her that were not stolen or looted. She was not imprisoned, and her children were not taken from her. A good many of López's associates and advisors survived, and again, they were generally treated well. A few were even admired for their courage and loyalty. That is somewhat difficult to understand in the 21st century when the consorts and associates of fallen dictators are often imprisoned or executed. The fate of common soldiers, women, and children among the camp followers was different; many starved and were poorly treated. Eliza, her children, and López's mother were members of the upper class and were treated gently.

There are other stories that may be true or may be fiction to tarnish López. When the Brazilian officers and soldiers found the tent

---

[82] Lillis, Michael. "The True Origins of Eliza Lynch." *The Irish Times*, March 11, 2014.

[83] Whigham, Thomas. *The Road to Armageddon: Paraguay Versus the Triple Alliance, 1864-1870*. Calgary, Alberta: University of Calgary Press, 2017, 412.

López had used, they were amazed at the quality of the furnishings. He still had cognac and good cigars, despite his small army going barefoot and malnourished. Those stories may be true, or they may be elaborations designed to fit the Brazilian narrative that the war was not against Paraguay or Paraguayans but the monster who ruled them.

The Paraguayan War caused hundreds of thousands of deaths, but there is no consensus as to how many. The overall losses in the war remain highly controversial. Brazil lost about 50,000 to 60,000 soldiers and sailors out of about 120,000 or more, with more of those deaths occurring due to disease rather than the battle. Argentina estimates that the Argentine dead range as high as eighteen thousand, but several thousand were due to rebellions within Argentina itself. There are estimates that as many as ten thousand Uruguayan soldiers died in the war. All three nations suffered civilian casualties, but the number is not known. Perhaps as many as five thousand civilians died as a consequence of the campaigns in Mato Grosso.

Paraguayan losses are also unknown, but they were extremely high, with estimates of 150,000 to more than 300,000 soldiers and civilians. The problem with assessing losses is that the population of Paraguay before the war started is asserted to be between 400,000 and more than a million. A majority of Paraguayan men lost their lives, with estimates as high as 90 percent of them being killed or dying of disease in the war. A very large percentage of the total Paraguayan prewar population died during the war. Paraguay probably lost at least a third of its population and perhaps more than half. In terms of the percentage of population lost, Paraguay compares with the losses of Poland and the Soviet Union in World War II, although the Paraguayan losses were a much higher percentage than either WWII country.

Conclusion – The Long Shadow of the Paraguayan War

When the war began in 1865, Argentine President Mitre boasted that the Allies would be in Asunción within three months. Instead, it took four years. Part of the problem for the Allies was the distance, as Asunción was hundreds of miles upriver. Part of the difficulty in winning the war was the excellent defense systems the Paraguayans had built and the fact that Paraguayan soldiers were almost always tenacious on defense. Some of the Allied commanders were ineffective, particularly some of the Brazilian commanders early in the war. Some had been given commands because of their aristocratic connections, not because of any evident competency. It took some hard fighting to discover who were the competent officers, and thousands of soldiers on both sides died because of tactical blunders.

That the Allies won a decisive victory did not eliminate tensions over Paraguay. Brazil and Argentina both suspected the other of desiring to annex all of Paraguay. Brazilian troops were stationed in Paraguay for several years, and Brazil almost completely dominated Paraguay well into the 1870s. The mutual suspicions came close to causing another war, and the Paraguayans managed to play Argentina and Brazil off each other, creating some space for independent actions.[84]

The war's shadow fell on the participants in different ways. Dom Pedro II, Brazil's second and last emperor, was ousted by a military coup in 1889. The emperor's reign was compromised by the issue of slavery, which ended in Brazil in 1888. Slaves who enlisted for service in the Paraguayan War were freed, and several thousand gained freedom that way. Slavery was becoming less profitable, and the moral case against slavery had become pervasive. When Brazilian slavery ended, the owners were not compensated.

The war was not fought in isolation from the rest of the world. Brazil managed to raise substantial loans from European bankers, including a £7 million loan arranged by the Rothschild bankers in Britain, which was used to purchase ironclads for the navy, among other weaponry. The British supplied weapons and were anxious for their domination of the La Plata trade. British warships also interfered with the Brazilian blockade at least three times to rescue trapped British subjects. Some historians of a Marxist bent blame the war on British capitalism.[85]

The regions Paraguay disputed with Argentina and Brazil were largely decided by the winners, and Paraguay lost more than fifty thousand square miles of its territory. The war did not end all territorial disputes: sizable chunks of the Chaco remained in dispute between Paraguay and Argentina. Somehow, the two decided to submit the dispute to arbitration, with the arbiter being the president of the United States, Rutherford Hayes. Hayes considered the dispute and eventually decided in favor of Paraguay. The arbitration decision was reluctantly accepted by Argentina but was wildly popular in Paraguay. The pleased Paraguayans named both a town and a district after Hayes.[86]

There was a sizable cultural consequence of the war. Cándido López, a soldier who lost his right arm at Curupayty, taught himself to

[84] Abente, Diego. "The War of the Triple Alliance: Three Explanatory Models." *Latin American Research Review* 22 (2), 1987. 64. JSTOR access, January 12, 2023.

[85] Bethell, Leslie. "The Paraguayan War 1864-70." Page 104 in Leslie Bethell, *Brazil: Essays on History and Politics*. London: University of London Press, 2018.

[86] Ibid, pg. 110.

paint with his left arm and became a notable painter in Buenos Aires. The war was reflected in a number of Brazilian and Argentinian books, including novels, poetry, and patriotic music. An opera, *Il Guarany*, by Antônio Carlos Gomes, one of the most famed South American composers of his century, premiered in Italy. The war resulted in an explosion of memoirs and histories, not least the work by Mitre, the president of Argentina and commander of the Allied forces for much of the war. The army became a powerful force in Brazilian politics, and veterans in both Argentina and Brazil dominated politics for many years.[87]

The dramatic scene of López defying the Brazilian patrol and his death, followed by Eliza Lynch burying him and her son with her bare hands, has become an iconic scene for patriotic Paraguayans. López is now usually seen as a patriot who led Paraguay against all odds. López was not Paraguay's last dictator.

The Brazilians did not harm Eliza. She was banned from Paraguay and took her surviving children back to France. She tried to recover her property or whatever of it she could. She was invited back to Paraguay by its president, and when she was promised that they would respect her, she returned. It did not go well, probably because she tried to claim property that had been given to her by her tyrant spouse. She was banished forever from Paraguay, went to Buenos Aires, and then returned to France. Eliza died there in 1886.

Francisco Solano López remained buried in the jungle for many years. His remains were brought back to Asunción in 1936 amid great patriotic celebrations. The remains were interred in the Pantheon of Heroes in the city. This was partly because Paraguay needed a shot of patriotism in the middle of the grueling Chaco War (1932–1935) with Bolivia, a bloody war that Paraguay won. The 1936 reinterment may have been an exercise in patriotism, but there seems little doubt that López was (and still is) seen as a Paraguayan national hero.

Criticism of López and his consort has become a cottage industry. The details in one account quite often contradict the details in another. One recent account claims that Eliza was a courtesan in France specializing in rich men and that when she was introduced to

---

[87] Ibid, pgs. 99-100.

López's mother, his mother nearly fainted and called for smelling salts. The account claims that Eliza was snubbed by the Asunción elite and referred to as *La Concubina Irlandesa*, although she allegedly got her revenge when her husband became dictator. She supposedly helped herself to jewels from the shrine of the Virgin of Carupe. The same account claims that when the bodies of López and their eldest son were brought to her, a Brazilian officer demanded she bury them both in the mud with her bare hands and that she spat at the officer. As a British citizen, she was immune from prosecution.[88]

Something about both López and his consort Eliza continues to draw interest. As this account shows, the facts of their relationship remain in dispute more than 150 years later. Whether López was a coward and whether Eliza was a greedy courtesan or the first lady of her adopted country may never be known for certain.

Eliza Lynch was buried in Paris after she died. Her body was brought back to Paraguay in the 1960s, and she was declared a national hero of Paraguay by yet another dictator, Alfredo Stroessner (1912–2006, r. 1954–1989). The current Paraguayan view of López and his consort is that they were heroes who fought against impossible odds, with a touch of Joan of Arc for Eliza. Aside from the convenience of having a patriotic dictator in the past to provide support for later Paraguayan tyrants like Stroessner, López is seen by many as the country's greatest hero.

In the decades following the end of the war in 1870, large numbers of Europeans migrated to Argentina and Brazil, while smaller numbers went to Uruguay and Paraguay. Migration from southern Italy was heavy, but there were also immigrants from Portugal, Spain, Germany, and smaller numbers of Arab migrants from the Middle East. An odd relationship exists between Paraguay and Lebanon and Syria because of that migration. Yerba mate has become mildly popular there because migrants returning to their homeland brought back a taste for the drink with them. Mate is now exported from

---

[88] Rogers, Rosemary. "Eliza Lynch: The Uncrowned Queen of Paraguay." *Irish American Magazine*, October-November 2014. https://www.irishamerica.com/2014/09/eliza-lynch-the-uncrowned-queen-of-paraguay-2/. Retrieved January 30, 2023.

Paraguay and Argentina to Lebanon and Syria.[89]

Paraguay took many years to recover from the war. Agriculture suffered from a severe loss of horses, mules, and cattle. The agricultural labor that had once been supplied by draft animals and men was replaced by women and boys. The very heavy losses of men meant that in some areas of the country, women heavily outnumbered them. Some historians think this resulted in an acceptance of women raising children outside of marriage and empowered women who had to replace men in agriculture and trade.

Other historians argue that Paraguayan history has predisposed the nation to authoritarian rulers. The Chaco War with Bolivia in the 1930s saw the patriotic glorification of Francisco Solano López, and the recent long rule of Alfredo Stroessner (r. 1954–1989) brought back the body of Eliza Lynch and acclaimed her as a national hero.

It is perhaps encouraging that the bloodiest war between nations in South American history was more than 150 years ago. The continent has seen far less death on the battlefield than in Europe or Asia. Perhaps the four nations learned something from their epic war.

---

[89] Wikipedia. "Yerba Mate." https://en.wikipedia.org/wiki/Yerba_mate . Retrieved January 22, 2023.

Here's another book by Captivating History that you might like

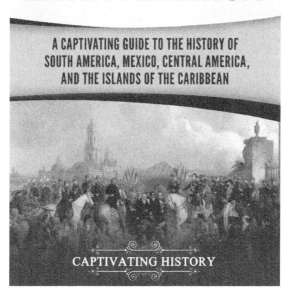

Free Bonus from Captivating History (Available for a Limited time)

Hi History Lovers!

Now you have a chance to join our exclusive history list so you can get your first history ebook for free as well as discounts and a potential to get more history books for free! Simply visit the link below to join.

Captivatinghistory.com/ebook

Also, make sure to follow us on Facebook, Twitter and Youtube by searching for Captivating History.

References

Abente, Diego. "The War of the Triple Alliance: Three Explanatory Models." *Latin American Research Review* 22 (2), 1987. 47-69. JSTOR access, January 12, 2023.

Alchetron. "Paraguayan War." https://alchetron.com/Paraguayan-War Retrieved January 13, 2023.

Bethell, Leslie. "The Paraguayan War 1864-70." Pages 93-112 in Leslie Bethell, *Brazil: Essays on History and Politics.* London: University of London Press, 2018.

Collmer, Robert. "Carlyle, Francia and Their Critics." Studies in Scottish Literature 14 (1), 1979. 1-12. https://scholarcommons.sc.edu/ssl/vol14/iss1/10/. Retrieved January 21, 2023.

Cooney, Jerry. "Paraguayan Independence and Dr. Francia." *Americas* 28 (4) April 1972. 407-28. JSTOR access June 28, 2023.

Ehlers, Hartmut. "The Paraguayan Navy, Past and Present." *Warship International* 41 (1), 2004. 79-97. JSTOR access, January 12, 2023.

Fioravanti, Carlos. "The Scourge of Disease During the Paraguayan War." *Pesquisa* Issue 309, 2021. https://revistapesquisa.fapesp.br/en/the-scourge-of-disease-during-the-paraguayan-war/Retrieved January 13, 2023.

Ganson, Barbara. "Following the Children into Battle: Women at War in Paraguay, 1864-1870." *The Americas* 46 (3), January 1990. 336-71. JSTOR access January 12, 2023.

Global Security.Org. "Cisplatine War, 1825-28." https://www.globalsecurity.org/military/world/war/cisplatine.htm Retrieved January 21, 2023.

Hanratty, Dana and Meditz, Sandra. *Paraguay: A Country Study.* Washington, DC: Library of Congress, 1988.

Heege, Robert. "War of the Triple Alliance: Bloodbath in Paraguay." January 2013. https://warfarehistorynetwork.com/article/war-of-the-triple-alliance-bloodbath-in-paraguay/Retrieved January 13, 2023.

Hudson, Rex and Meditz, Sandra. *Uruguay: A Country Study.* Washington, DC, 1990. Library of Congress.

Kennedy, Thomas. *Jose Gaspar Rodriguez de Francia and Francisco Solano López, as Historical Heroes.* Thesis, Texas Tech University, 1974.

Lillis, Michael. "The True Origins of Eliza Lynch." *The Irish Times,* March 11, 2014.

Military History. "The Mato Grosso Campaign." https://military-history.fandom.com/wiki/Mato_Grosso_CampaignRetrieved January 24, 2023.

Military History. "Paraguayan War." https://military-history.fandom.com/wiki/Paraguayan_WarRetrieved January 13, 2023.

Military History. "Naval Battle of Riachuelo." Retrieved January 27, 2023.

Omniatlas. "South America 1864: Outbreak of the Paraguayan War." Also maps South America 1865, 1866, 1867, 1868, 1869 and 1870. https://omniatlas.com/maps/south-america/18641213/Retrieved January 11, 2023.

Penalta, Alfredo Fornos. "Draft Dodgers, War Resisters, and Turbulent Gauchos: The War of the Triple Alliance Against Paraguay." *Americas* 38 (4) April 1982. 463-79. JSTOR access January 28, 2023.

Rahmeier, Clarissa Sanfelice. "The Materiality of Cultural Encounters in the *Treinta Pueblos de la Missiones.*" Pages 69-88 in Linda A. Nelson, ed., *Cultural Worlds of the Jesuits in Colonial Latin America.* London: University of London Press, 2020.

Redington, Erick. "The Paraguayan President Who Brought His Country to Military Catastrophe." *History is Now Magazine* online. https://www.historyisnowmagazine.com/ blog/2021/11/22/the -paraguayan-president/. Parts 1, 2, 3 and 4. Retrieved January 13, 2023.

Rogers, Rosemary. "Eliza Lynch: The Uncrowned Queen of Paraguay." *Irish American Magazine,* October-November 2014. https://www.irishamerica.com/2014/09/eliza-lynch-the-uncrowned-queen-of-paraguay-2/. Retrieved January 30, 2023.

Shipping Wonders of the World. "Rio de la Plata." https://www.shippingwondersoftheworld.com/river_plate.htmlRetrieved January 14, 2023.

War of the Triple Alliance. Com. "War of the Triple Alliance" internet site. https://warofthetriplealliance.com/Retrieved January 13, 2023.

Warren, Gaylord. "The Paraguayan Image of the War of the Triple Alliance." *The Americas* 19 (1), July 1962. 3-20. JSTOR access January 12, 2023.

Warren, Harris. "Roberto Adolfo Chodasiewicz: A Polish Soldier of Fortune in the Paraguayan War." *The Americas* 41 (3), January 1985. 1-19. JSTOR access January 12, 2023.

Weisiger, Alex. *Logics of War: Explanations for Limited and Unlimited Conflicts.* New York: Cornell University Press, 2013. Chapter 3: "War to the Death in Paraguay." 86-104.

Whigham, Thomas. "Brazil's Balloon Corps. Pride, Desperation and the Limits of Military Intelligence in the Triple Alliance War." *Luso-Brazilian Review* 52 (2), 2015. 1-18. JSTOR access January 12, 2023.

Whigham, Thomas. *The Paraguayan War: Causes and Early Conduct*, 2nd Edition. Calgary, Alberta: University of Calgary Press, 2018.

Whigham, Thomas. *The Road to Armageddon: Paraguay Versus the Triple Alliance, 1864-1870.* Calgary, Alberta: University of Calgary Press, 2017.

Wikipedia. "Eliza Lynch (1833-1886)." https://en.wikipedia.org/wiki/Eliza_LynchRetrieved January 13, 2023.

Wikipedia. "Yerba Mate." https://en.wikipedia.org/wiki/Yerba_mateRetrieved January 22, 2023.

Wikiwand. "Fortress of Humaitá." /.https://www.wikiwand.com/en/Humait%C3%A1 Retrieved January 24, 2023.

Williams, John. "The Undrawn Line: Three Centuries of Strife on the Paraguayan- Mato Grosso Border." *Luso-Brazilian Studies* 17 (1), Summer 1980. 17-40. JSTOR access January 24, 2023.

Printed in Great Britain
by Amazon

27198347R00066